ALONE

ALONE

Emotional, legal and financial help
for the widowed or divorced woman

Helen Antoniak   Nancy Scott   Nancy Worcester

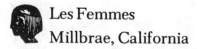

Les Femmes
Millbrae, California

Published by Les Femmes Publishing
231 Adrian Road
Millbrae, California 94030

First printing, February 1979
Made in the United States of America

Cover design: Robert Hu

Library of Congress Cataloging in Publication Data

Antoniak, Helen, 1947-
    Alone.

    Bibliography: p.
    Includes index.
    1. Widows—United States—Handbooks, manuals etc.
2. Divorcees—United States—Handbooks, manuals, etc.
I.   Scott, Nancy L., 1942-   joint author.
II.   Worcester, Nancy, 1944-   joint author
III.   Title.
HQ1058.5.U5A57 1979   301.42'8   78-61612
ISBN 0-89087-933-8

    2 3 4 5 6 7 — 85 84 83 82 81 80 79

To all who have loved me and helped me grow,
this book is a fruit of your love.

Helen Antoniak

In memory of my father, and in deep
appreciation to my best friend, my mother.

Nancy Lynch Scott

I dedicate this book to Hadley Worcester, my
daughter, who gave as much as we did; to Susan
Dunn, Susan Golding and John Worcester for
being with me; and to women everywhere, for
what they are and what they can be.

Nancy Worcester

CONTENTS

PREFACE

We will begin this preface with a story that poses a riddle-like question. If the tale seems familiar to you, you may have heard it on the television series, "All in The Family."

One day a man and his son were involved in a serious automobile accident. The man was pronounced dead at the scene of the accident and the boy was rushed to the nearest hospital. The doctor in the emergency room of the hospital examined the boy and found that he needed immediate surgery. The doctor, who was fully capable of operating, announced, "I cannot operate on this boy because he is my son!"

Now, the question is "Who is the doctor?" While you are mulling it around in the back of your mind, we will proceed. We are writing this book because we felt a great need for it. We were constantly being asked the same questions over and over and had no single resource book to recommend. There are certain questions that continually arise in the minds of the suddenly single women with whom we each work. "How do I find a good attorney?" "What should I do with our credit cards?" "Do I need a will?" Underlying the voiced questions are the very personal and worrisome ones. "Am I going crazy?" "Why do I feel like I cannot handle money?"

If you are asking some of these questions, we have written this book for you. If you are not yet asking these questions but feel there may be a divorce or death in the future, this book is for you, too.

This book may cause you to examine a path you will never personally walk. If all we do is shed light on that path, we have fulfilled our purpose. We hope that your purpose in reading this book is to acquire knowledge. Ironically, if you are right now in the throes of widowhood or divorce, the emotional turmoil you are probably experiencing will make it difficult to concentrate on any book. Hopefully, this book will be the helping hand that you use to pull yourself up. At the end we have also included a resource list of many other books which you may find helpful.

Now, back to the riddle. Did you guess that the doctor had to be the boy's mother? If, like so many, you automatically assumed that the doctor had to be a man, the riddle was a tough one.

We have done something a bit unusual in this book, which we hope will ride heavily on those automatic assumptions that professionals are male. We have departed from traditional English grammar and sometimes used the feminine pronoun when referring to any person you might find yourself dealing with: attorneys, counselors, insurance sales people, escrow officers, creditors, etc. We took this bold step for a variety of reasons. (If you don't feel it is a bold step, just wait and see if those pronouns don't leap at you!)

First of all, people have a tendency to fall into conventional thinking when it comes to jobs and sexual stereotyping. When you are seeking help with the myriad of problems that being suddenly single brings with it, you need to consider helpers of both sexes. You might really be limiting your field if you don't. There might even be some strong reasons that you would prefer to deal with someone of your own sex at this time of crisis. Besides encouraging you to think of the possibility of seeking help from someone of your own sex, we had yet another very important reason for pushing this concept of females in such positions. You may soon be facing the job market for the first time or you may be looking for advancement. When you keep seeing those "her's" and "she's" in all those different careers, we hope a light will go on somewhere in your brain. You'll say to yourself, "If she can do it, so can I!"

ACKNOWLEDGMENTS

The authors wish to gratefully acknowledge the following experts for their professional advice in assembling the factual material for this book.

BONNIE N. READING, attorney at law, for her invaluable assistance with the chapter on divorce entitled "Getting Out Gracefully." Ms. Reading wishes to acknowledge the assistance of Christina Mills and Barbara Reusch.

WILLIAM J. BRIERTON, JR., attorney at law, for his invaluable assistance with the chapter on widowhood entitled "What Every Woman Should Know."

DIANE SULLIVAN, attorney at law, for her invaluable assistance with the chapter on credit entitled "Where Credit Is Due."

KENNETH BOHLANDER, C.P.C.U. and JAMES O. REYNOLDS for their invaluable assistance with the chapter on insurance entitled "When to Take Coverage."

J. DOUGLASS JENNINGS, JR., attorney at law, for his invaluable assistance with the chapter on estate planning entitled "You Can't Take It With You But Your Heirs May Think You Did."

The authors also wish to acknowledge the help of the following friends and advisors: Peter G. Aylward, attorney at law; Leslie M. Crouch, attorney at law; Linda Chester, literary agent; Renée Klepesch, probate paralegal; David Monahan, attorney at law; Howard Potash, attorney at law; Edith Reid, C.L.U.; Bonnie Stringer-Tarnow, Widowed to Widowed administrative assistant; Ann Sturgis, Director of

Stress Management Training Institute; and the entire Board of Directors of the San Diego Widowed to Widowed Program, Inc. A portion of the proceeds from this book benefits the Widowed to Widowed Program.

We wish to express special thanks and appreciation to Gloria Jacobs, our manuscript editor and typist.

Finally we would like to thank Joycelyn Moulton, our editor and Celestial Arts/Les Femmes Publishing.

ALONE

Good Grief! What's happening to me?

Life would be simple if we could compartmentalize our lives so that we would be working on only one problem at a time. Unfortunately, while in the throes of widowhood or divorce, a person must wrestle with huge problems in many of life's arenas.

The transition from being married to being single is not an easy one. What complicates the divorce and probate proceedings and the legal and financial decisions which precede and follow these actions, are *emotions*. This first chapter is directed at the emotions—how to understand them, how to sort them out, how to make sure you are not making less than rational decisions because of them. The end of a relationship is not just a legal and financial matter. Few women avoid the emotional consequences of separation. What is that horrible feeling in the pit of one's stomach?

We will focus on an emotion not really understood or even used much in American society today. It's a five letter word called *grief*. Generally, the word grief is only associated with a death. Actually, we all go through many griefs. The problem is that most people do not understand what is happening emotionally and they suffer because of their lack of understanding.

Basically, grief is the normal reaction to a disappointment. Heaven knows we all have a lot of disappointments in our lives! Generally, we are able to pick ourselves up when we

1

Alone

are knocked down. When something is taken from us, we find something else. But when some*one* is taken from us, particularly the most important person in our lives, the recovery is not nearly so easy or so swift.

This may seem very obvious for the woman who loses her lifelong mate in a sudden, tragic death. Other less obvious but still very strong griefs also deserve our attention.

Divorce may end a marriage that was happy for many years. A death may end a marriage that was very stormy and unpleasant. The end of a marriage may mean the end of many more things than just a relationship between two people. *All* the "endings" must be grieved.

If the complex grief process were to be described very simply, we might say, "Grief is saying 'goodbye' in order to be able to say 'hellos' "! The problem is that the majority of us have difficulty saying goodbye. Some of us go to great lengths to avoid acknowledging the start of a separation. We avoid the last goodbye to people moving away. We disappear when the fellow employee is making the last rounds at the office. We don't like the thought of losing someone or something, especially when we know it will be forever.

Besides the difficulty of saying goodbye, many people have problems knowing just *what it is* they are saying goodbye to.

As strange as it may sound, one of the big problems with grief is that people often do not know *what they are grieving*. Widows and divorcees will attempt to pull themselves together and not give in to tears by saying, "I know I'm just feeling sorry for myself. No self-pity for me!"

At first this tactic has a nice, healthy ring to it. After all, who likes to be around a "cry baby." The problem is that a person who has had her dreams shattered has a right, even an *obligation*, to cry. Remember! The definition of grief is saying goodbye in order to say new hellos.

To really grieve, constructively, a person needs to be in touch with *every aspect of the loss*. The end of a relationship through either death or divorce means the end to many habits, feelings and future plans. The loss of "being married" is in itself a blow to many women whose teenage dreams al-

2

ways centered around a husband. The plans of traveling across the country next summer in the camper must also be grieved. The plans for retiring and growing old together are suddenly gone. Now your hidden, almost forgotten, expectations can never be realized.

Similar to future dreams which will never be achieved may be past expectations that were not fulfilled. Perhaps you did not have the children you had hoped for or the business did not produce anticipated profits. Maybe you sacrificed the dream of a custom-built home or lived for many years in a part of the country you detested. Now that it's all over, you may suddenly find yourself feeling cheated about things you willingly sacrificed at the time. Those sacrifices hardly seemed to bother you then. You had easily said those good-byes because you were convinced that other good things were just around the corner. Now, those good things haven't materialized and it is too late to make those choices again.

Everytime you realize another aspect of your shattered dream, you should shed tears for it. You must take the time to examine all the angles, all the possibilities of your loss. You need to know *what it is you are saying goodbye to.*

Similar to our aversion to acknowledging a separation by saying goodbye, is our reluctance to show when we are in pain. It is now common knowledge that many men get ulcers because they were raised in an environment that shamed masculine tears. Even the legitimate tears of a little boy who skins his knee are stifled. Similarly, girls receive a message that tears are a sign of feminine weakness or a weapon to manipulate "non-cryers!"

Too many people have learned how to endure losses with a sort of tearless stoicism and to endure pain without acknowledging it. Even though we avoid the formal goodbye, the loss is there nonetheless. Since a complainer is an unwelcome member of a group, some people take pride in this ability to appear as if losses don't bother them.

This non-grieving approach to life would be fine except for one flaw—when we cannot bring ourselves to say "goodbye," we cannot say new "hellos." Consciously or unconsciously, we begin to take the attitude immortalized in a popular song, "I'll never fall in love again."

The first reaction to a death or the realization that a divorce is imminent is disbelief. This is similar to what we go through on a small scale when we lose something relatively insignificant. We will look in the spot we think we last saw it again and again. We retrace our steps, we examine all possibilities. We enlist others in our search, saying, "I can't believe I lost it."

A similar searching process goes on with the loss of a relationship. Obviously, if we were really convinced that something was lost forever, we would not keep searching for it. Not only do we consciously review the process that brought about the loss, but subconsciously we wrestle with a reality we simply cannot accept. Thus it is that widows dream their husbands are alive and it was all just a mix-up at the hospital. Divorcees, too, retreat to memories of better times, searching endlessly for reasons "why."

One of the distinct differences between divorce and widowhood is the finality. A divorcee may spend much of her energy hoping there will be a miraculous turnaround in the situation. Her children, too, may make efforts to reunite their parents. This fantasy is not only very unrealistic, but its emotional ambivalence will prolong the grief process. Even though there are statistics that do support the fact that some people marry each other for a second time, it is still much healthier to grieve now and accept the turnaround, if it does come, as a brand new relationship.

Some people will go into a form of withdrawal after the hurt of a loss. Many women find that while their thoughts and emotions are in a numb sort of fog, their bodies function on "automatic pilot." Later they look back with no recollection of what they said or did. This is certainly not a good time for big legal and financial decisions! A widow who is feeling unloved and believes that there is no hope for the future is quite likely to give things away—clothes and jewelry—even big things like cars and real estate. Similarly, a divorcee may take very little interest in the division of the property during her divorce.

If this numbed, apathetic stage is bewildering, the next one can be frightening. There is a natural tendency to strike back after being wounded. Such "unladylike" feelings as bitterness, resentment and hostility may arise. If it is a mistake for a divorcee to hope for a magical reconciliation, it is even a worse mistake for her to hope to wreak revenge because of feelings of bitterness, hostility and resentment. Just the opposite of a widow who gives everything away without a second thought is the divorcee who tries to get her hands on everything to avenge her hurt. This can be particularly tragic when the custody of children is suddenly seized upon as a tool for punishment or extortion.

Again, it is necessary to stress that we are talking about a normal grief process. We may like to think we are not the "type" to become hostile, bitter or resentful. But it is a normal reaction that many people have when their egos suffer a crushing blow. We might even take this further and say it is a healthy reaction. The unhealthy reaction is for people to internalize their anger and become depressed, even to the point of suicide. The difficult part of the problem is not just the feelings, but remaining objective in your financial and legal dealings when you are experiencing these feelings.

Another stage along this uphill road called grief is *guilt*. All of us have done things in our lives which familiarized us with that awful, gnawing feeling commonly labeled "guilt." Usually, the feeling first came when someone pointed out the error of our ways and we were punished. With widowhood and divorce, there is very often a feeling of being punished. We ask ourselves, "Why did this happen to me?" or "What did I do to deserve this?" Then, being the human beings we are, it is not hard to muster up past deeds which might provide grounds for guilt. These offenses may range from the "if onlys" ("if only" I had insisted that he watch his diet; "if only" we had seen a marriage counselor in time. . .) to the more serious "I shouldn't have drunk so heavily" or "I shouldn't have told him about that affair."

As if it were not enough for us to dredge up incidents from the past and examine them for motivations and deeds which merit feelings of guilt, we also look to the present circumstances as something to feel guilty about. After all, aren't we rotten to be feeling bitter, hostile and resentful? The divorcee looks at her children and says, "I am depriving you of a full-time father." The widow may actually be relieved that after a long, grueling, expensive illness, her husband finally died. She then has grounds for feeling guilty for feeling relieved. The cycle can go on and on. People will say"You shouldn't feel that way," but it won't help. You are feeling punished and worthy of that punishment; therefore you are guilty, guilty, guilty.

What does one do with guilt? There isn't much in our society to really help us deal with guilt. Sometimes, a widow and her family may spend an inordinate amount of money on a funeral in an attempt to expiate guilt. (The funeral industry does not seem to feel guilty about cashing in on somebody else's guilt.) Others may spend money talking to counselors about it. Direct ways to make amends are gone. You cannot live your life over. A few people will become great humanitarians to make up some past wrong. If bandaging lepers in some steaming jungle will help relieve your burden of guilt, the lepers will be glad to have you. If donating money to a worthy cause will do it for you, the Widowed to Widowed Program will cheerfully accept your donation.

What is important to understand about guilt is that there is both real guilt and unreal guilt. When you are the one feeling guilty, it may be impossible to distinguish what type of guilt you have. Real guilt is what you should be feeling if you did something rotten. Unreal guilt is searching for any normal day to day behavior and branding it as rotten since that is how you are feeling. Especially when somebody suddenly dies, it is easy to do an analytical rerun on your last interactions with the person and find yourself less than perfect. To say that it was this imperfection which hastened the demise is unreal grounds for guilt. In an extreme circumstance such as suicide, it is really hard for a person not to take on the entire burden of guilt. "It was my fault, just as surely as if I had pulled the trigger," a person may say. In reality, each person is responsible for herself. If you are thoroughly agreeing with this, you have gotten the only real answer there can be for guilt.

So far, we have been talking about the emotions which begin erupting like a volcano following a separation. This is one aspect of grief. Another is the tension that this emotional experience can bring. The layperson is now becoming familiar with the concept of "future shock" and the stress that change has on one's life. Popular magazine and newspaper articles have given people score sheets to evaluate the total amount of changes they have experienced and the point value that psychology professionals have equated with these changes.

Widowhood and divorce are at the top of the list of life events which cause a person great stress. Unfortunately, very few lives are free from additional stresses which come along as "side effects" of a death or divorce. Although it is not guaranteed, there is a strong likelihood that if you go through many life changes in a short period of time, you will become emotionally or physically ill. This does not mean that if you find one of these "tests" and score yourself extremely high, you are entitled to a nervous breakdown. A high score is a warning to take better care of yourself and try to avoid additional changes.

When anyone is in an uncomfortable spot, there is a natural inclination to try to get out of it. Thus, the unpleasant change of widowhood or divorce may prompt you to run. Your thought is, "a trip to Europe, a boyfriend, a new neighborhood, different furniture, and everything will be all right. This horrible feeling will go away." Unfortunately, everything will not be all right and the feeling may get worse rather than better. The stress of additional changes could bring you to your first stay in a mental hospital.

It would be marvelous if we could simply change our

names, move to a different city and start life all over again. We are not so much a product of our environment as we are of our dreams and aspirations. If we do not face our grief, and say our goodbyes, we are simply unable to take the stress of new hellos. We cannot enter a second door until we exit from the first. If we try to do this, we face impossible stress. This is why it is so important to slow down and examine what we are doing very carefully. The more you feel the desperate urge to flee, the more important it probably is that you stay put. You have been hurt. You have suffered a blow. You must, sooner or later, go through the natural grief process, unpleasant as it is. The best choice you can make is to go through it naturally, know you are going through it, and rejoice when you realize that it is mostly behind you.

While the grief process is difficult, do not look at the outcome as bleak. If you are going through the roughest situation you have ever been through in your whole life, you are bound to come out wiser and more mature than you were before. You can make the best of a bad situation and not only come out of it as an emotionally healthy woman but one who is better equipped to handle the problems of life than those who have only experienced smooth sailing. The secret of this growth is understanding yourself and how to handle the multitude of problems.

The best way to understand yourself is to have people to interact with and especially to use as a sounding board. For many of us, the term "best friend" is a concept that ended with grammar school. Usually, it fell quite naturally that your husband was supposed to be your "best friend" and now that he is gone, you have no one to lean on. Now is the time you need a friend or "confidant" like never before. You need someone you can call at two in the morning and know you will not be rebuffed. You need to have a sympathetic ear that you can rant and rave to and know that what you say will go no further. It is up to you *who* you choose as a confidant. You may want someone of the same sex or you may know that, for you, it must be someone of the opposite sex.

You may feel most comfortable talking to a relative, or on the other hand, any member of the family may be the *last* you would confide in. Age and education does not matter. What matters is that this person care about you and be willing to listen without criticism or unwanted advice. You may choose a person that you get together with often for dinner, jogging or bridge. Or it may be someone who only fills this listening role. The point is that you need at least one person, preferably more, that you know you can lean on while you grow.

If your search for such a person is fruitless, or if your problems seem too much for both of you, it is time to seek professional help. You may never have sought out such help in the past, and you may never need to in the future, but *now is the time* when you need professional help.

Just as there are many factors which may or may not be important to you when you are selecting a friend, there may be important criteria to use in selecting a counselor. It may be very important that the person be older or of the opposite sex. You may have some reason why you would only consider seeing a psychiatrist or a social worker. A pastoral counselor might be the first or last person you seek out. Perhaps there is a particular approach to your problem which you would want this counselor to have. If you just read a book on transactional analysis, you may be convinced that this is the only way you want to look at what you are experiencing. The issue is not so much whom you go to or what approach you want to use. The issue is that you grow. Grief is painful and the growth that it brings may be painful. It is very important that you select and continue to see a counselor who seems sincerely concerned with you and is sensitive to your pain, someone who will see you through this time of difficulty.

It is not easy to select a counselor. You may want to examine licensing procedures and referral methods in your community. You may ask your doctor or clergy for a referral. Perhaps one of your friends can tell you of someone they believe is good. It is important that you know right from the start what you hope to receive from your counseling and how much you are willing to pay for it. You are looking for someone you are not afraid to be honest with, so you had better begin with clear communication about what goals you would like to set for yourself and how you wish to use the expertise of the counselor to help you achieve those goals. How much money is it worth for you to have help with your emotional problems?

One of the interesting things about paying money for emotional help is that money is such an emotional topic in and of itself. It should rank above sex, religion and politics as a subject not to be discussed at the dinner table. If you even suggest to someone that they have a hangup about money, they will immediately get emotional. Money is so much more than just printed paper used in exchange for goods and services. Somehow we unconsciously look at money as mother's milk and future security. While we do not like to believe we are attached to money, it is an essential part of our very existence.

While it is impossible to be objective about money, it is important that we spend some time sorting out the emotional messages that money sends to us. Later in this book, there will be financially sound advice which may be very much contrary to your emotional framework. Pause and appreciate what is happening to you. You may very likely continue on with the same financial policies that you previously followed but at least be cognizant of the emotional factors which cause you to do what you do.

This chapter has talked about the bubbling volcano of emotions that is coming from within. We have not even begun to touch on all the pressures which people are making from without. Advice, good and bad, is coming at you from all directions. It is easy to feel pressured and want to please everybody rather than to follow your own instincts. Somehow, you may think you would not be in this situation if you had followed someone's good advice sooner.

Instead of listening to the advice itself, stop and consider the source. Why are they giving you this advice? What advantage would it be to them if you followed their advice? Are they exerting pressure on you to act more quickly than you want to act? Even if you follow good advice, if you feel uncomfortable doing it, it is not good.

We have hardly mentioned children. If you have children, especially if they are living with you, read this entire chapter over again as if you were in their shoes. What are they saying goodbye to? For one thing, they are saying goodbye to the old you. No matter how you try to keep things the same, you are not the same, and this experience has changed the course of your children's lives as well as your own. While children do have remarkable recovery powers, it is important that you consider their needs at this time of crisis, too. If you need others to come in and lend a hand, ask for the children's sake. Children need to be reassured they are still loved and they did not cause the awful thing which may have occurred, and that somehow they will be all right and will be provided for no matter what happens.

While you are instilling faith in the future in your children, you may rekindle some hope for the future in your own heart. There is a high probability that there is another marriage in your future. It is not too soon to start thinking about that. What you must ask yourself is how much will you have adjusted and grown before you enter into that new relationship. What qualities would you be seeking in a future mate? Women who rise to a new level of independence and maturity seek a different style marriage than they had the first time around. Too often women who feel they cannot face life alone fall into a relationship with the "wrong man at the right time." She is vulnerable and he is supportive. While it is comfortable for awhile, the woman eventually regains her footing and then feels obligated to a man that she would be crazy to marry.

Grief is not a time for big decisions, including the one of permanent commitment. So, draw back, and list your own qualities as well as the qualities of your "Prince Charming." Your personal qualities are the assets you will be able to offer a new relationship and your list will grow as you do. If the time comes when he shows up, you will be ready for him. If that day never comes, you are still the winner since you have grown through grief and have come to love your own good qualities.

Can your legal eagle fly?

Lawyers, like doctors, are specialists. Women are usually accustomed to selecting a medical specialist for a particular problem. You may have a pediatrician for your children, an obstetrician/gynecologist for yourself, and a general practitioner or doctor of internal medicine for your husband. You may even be accustomed to visiting a clinic comprised of a number of specialists. Choosing an attorney is very similar to choosing a doctor; but you may not be used to looking at lawyers in the same way. Somehow health seems to traditionally fall into the wife's domain, while the husband concerns himself with the legal and financial matters. Many women have never had to seek legal advice before.

If you are close to widowhood or divorce right now, one of your very real concerns will be choosing the right attorney for your situation. You will need a lawyer who is a specialist, and the prerequisites for a divorce attorney as opposed to a probate attorney vary greatly. The best way to find a good lawyer is the same way you find a good doctor. You simply ask around. Perhaps you have a friend who has just gone through a divorce or perhaps you know a widow whose husband's estate has recently been probated. If your friend was pleased with her attorney and you respect your friend's opinion, you may wish to consult the same lawyer.

When you are looking for a *divorce* attorney, it is important for you to remember that you need someone whose viewpoint is as objective as possible. You will be best represented by someone who has professional concern for your problem but who is not involved with you or your husband either socially or emotionally. This means that if you have a friend or relative who is a lawyer, you should not ask that person to represent you. (If you ask her, she or anyone in her firm should refuse to take the case.) Instead, ask her to recommend three attorneys whose reputations she personally respects.

If you are looking for a *probate* attorney, the opposite suggestion would hold true. You will be best represented by an attorney who knows as much as possible about you, your husband and your husband's business affairs. This means that an attorney in the family or a family friend would be ideal. If your husband employed an attorney in the regular course of his business, this person would probably also be ideal. If this attorney does not do probate work himself, perhaps another member of his firm does. Again, if that does not work out, you may always ask this person for the names of attorneys whose reputations he respects.

If your attempts to find a lawyer through personal recommendations fail, most communities have referral services which are maintained by the lawyers themselves. You will find these listed in the telephone directory. Referral services differ from community to community. Some have stringent requirements on the attorneys they will list, such as standards for the amount of experience in a particular area and length of time in practice. Others will list any attorney who has been admitted to practice law. Some services list by special areas of practice, such as divorce or probate; others do not list by specialty. It would be very good for you to find out beforehand what criteria are used in the particular service you are consulting and weigh your decisions accordingly. Many referral services are set up so that the attorneys whose names you are given charge only a minimal amount for the first consultation. This should be an advantage in allowing you to compare attorneys at a relatively low cost. However, some services don't work this way; so you should find out ahead of time what fees will be charged.

There is yet another way you may wish to go about finding an attorney. There is a set of volumes called the Martindale-Hubbell Law Directory. These reference books are available at any law library and at most public libraries. Attorneys are listed by state and city. After each attorney's name you will find his or her educational background. You will also find a rating. Capital "A" is the highest and then, of course, there are "B's" and "C's." These ratings are given to an attorney by other attorneys in the community who are rated either "A" or "B." The rating system is biased to favor length of practice. This doesn't necessarily make an attorney better, but at least it may give you a starting point. There is also a sort of "yellow pages" directory in the back of each volume where an attorney can pay to be listed. This selection contains a brief biography including the attorney's educational background, honors received, and perhaps areas of specialty.

You may have been aware that lawyers were not allowed to list an area of specialization with their names in the yellow pages of the telephone book. The legal Canon of Ethics has recently been changed. Now, in some states, attorneys can identify the areas of law they feel most competent or interested in practicing. This new privilege is no more or no less helpful than similar listings for physicians. If you have no other recourse, this is a place to start.

In view of the fact that thirty to fifty percent of the students now enrolled in law school are women, the number of women attorneys will increase tremendously in the very near future. Whether you would honestly prefer a male or female is an important criterion to consider when choosing an attorney. It is a matter of personal preference and should be given very careful thought. There may be times for divorcees when a person of the opposite sex will, by no other reason than virtue of being of the opposite sex, be a deterrent to your ability to work with that person. On the other hand, some widows may feel much more confident having a man handle their le-

gal and financial affairs which were previously handled by
their husbands. Whatever the case with you, you will be
much better off if you make a conscious choice rather than
choosing a man because you always think of lawyers as
males.

Another factor to consider in choosing an attorney is the
size of the law firm with which he or she is associated. Depending on where you live, a firm is usually considered large
if it has thirteen to fifteen lawyers. Yet, in a metropolitan area, large firms can have more than a hundred lawyers. A
large firm is likely to have a specialist in your area of concern, but much of the work on your case may be done by an
associate rather than by the partner you first consult. "Asso-
ciates" are usually younger, less experienced lawyers who
have not yet become partners in the firm. In a small firm you
are likely to get more personal attention, but the lawyer may
not be a specialist in any particular area.

We cannot overemphasize the importance of having a
good rapport with your attorney. When you go through divorce or probate, you can expect to spend a minimum of six
months to one year working closely with your attorney—
sometimes this is much longer. Your lawyer will be handling
extremely personal matters for you at a time when you are
under great emotional and perhaps financial stress. Her advice, and the manner in which she handles the legal aspects
of your divorce or probate, will have a significant effect on
your future security and peace of mind.

Any lawyer is professionally and ethically bound to represent you to the best of his ability. But we all know, as with
any profession, not all lawyers are equally gifted or dedicat-
ed. Nor will each person be equally suited to your personal
needs. Here are some things to consider.

Your divorce attorney should be someone who will see that
your interests and desires are fairly represented. He must
help you in sorting out the facts of your case and present
these facts as skillfully as possible in negotiating with your
husband's attorney or before a judge. For these reasons you

need someone with litigation skill—the more courtroom experience the better. He should strike you as someone who is fair and reasonable. You should determine his skill at negotiation. If it is not possible to do this by obervation, see if you can do it at least by reputation. Sometimes it is not possible to find a good litigator who is also a good negotiator. Some lawyers are hardly satisfied unless there is a "fight to the finish" in court; others are more naturally skilled at negotiation and compromise. Try to make your decision based on whether or not *you* want to, or think you will *have* to, fight hard in court, or whether you would prefer to settle things with your spouse outside of court and think you may be able to with the help of the right attorney.

Depending on the size and complexity of the property involved, you will also want to assess the attorney's financial and tax ability. Is she also a Certified Public Accountant (CPA)? Does she use CPA's as consultants? Is she, herself, a tax expert or does she have a tax expert in her law firm to consult? What are the largest divorce cases she has recently handled and what was the outcome? Expect general but honest answers.

There are also a few things you should *not* be looking for in your attorney. One of these is psychological help or counseling. An attorney is not trained as a therapist. Do not expect him to help you thread your way through significant emotional problems. Attempting to use your attorney in this way is a waste of his time and your money. It is also a little like going to your family physician for investment counseling. You will not be doing your attorney or yourself justice by expecting his psychological guidance because the best service he can give you is to remain fair, objective and as reasonable as possible and to insist that *you* try to approach your problems this way, too. If you find that your emotions are getting the better of you, it's time to seek help from a professional counselor. There are psychiatrists, psychologists, social workers, marriage and family counselors and pastors trained in this area and ready to help.

If you should not look to your attorney for psychological counseling, you should certainly not look at her as your personal weapon or vindicator. To expect her to "get" your husband or to self-righteously uphold your viewpoint on petty grievances between you and your husband is not realistic. Besides this, it would be very unhealthy on your part. Many lawyers simply refuse to handle divorce cases where bitterness is so extreme. It is best to vent your spleen elsewhere and get your attorney to spend her time on the real legal business at hand.

While the widow may read the above paragraph with relief that she will not be tempted to use her attorney as a weapon or vindicator, she must constantly bear in mind that she cannot look to her attorney as a grief counselor or a husband substitute. The probate attorney should be someone who will guide the widow confidently in managing her husband's estate and carrying out the dictates of the law. He will help execute the will, if the decedent expressed his wishes in a will, and will also help complete any unfinished business affairs. When it comes to looking for a probate attorney, the three most important things to look for are experience, experience, and experience.

Now that we have given you some suggestions on *what* to look for in an attorney, we would like to tell you how to do your own comparison shopping. Many people end up being represented by the first attorney they talk to simply because they think that is how the selection process works. Perhaps you didn't realize that *you* can interview an attorney to determine if you would like him to represent you.

Before you begin your "legal shopping," gather the names of at least three different attorneys who have been recommended through any of the methods we have suggested. You must then proceed to interview each one of them and pick the one that you feel will do the best job representing you. When you request your first appointment with each lawyer, make it clear to the secretary and to the lawyer that you are considering several attorneys and that you wish to consult her on this basis. Right then, you should also determine if there will be a fee for this initial visit and, if so, how much. Your initial conference is a good time to practice assertiveness. *You* are interviewing the *attorney* and there are lots of things you need to know in order to make a decision on whether you wish to hire that attorney.

If you are considering a divorce, ask what percentage of this attorney's practice is in divorce. Explain your goals to the attorney and ask his opinion. Does he think your expectations are realistic? How will he help you attain them? Later on in this chapter you will find guidelines to help you establish your legal goal.

Whether you have come in for assistance in divorce or probate, you should also ask the attorney to describe the legal process involved and to estimate the time schedule required. Be sure to come to the interview equipped with a notebook and a list of the questions or subjects you wish to discuss. Write notes on the answers. Ask the attorney whether she will handle your case personally or through paralegals and office help. Also ask whether she will personally appear in the divorce court if this is necessary.

A most important area to discuss right at the beginning with the attorney is her fees. In probate, fees are set by the state on a percentage basis and total charges will depend largely on the size of your husband's estate. While there are statutory minimums for most attorneys' fees, such extraordinary costs as litigation, tax returns or the unusual efforts expended in the sale of property and other details can and probably should be negotiated. The point is, *you* are employing the attorney and should not be surprised by the bill.

While probate fees are established by statute, divorce fees vary greatly. Some lawyers charge a "flat fee," usually several hundred dollars. Other attorneys charge an hourly rate ranging from thirty-five to several hundred dollars depending on where you live and the skill or reputation of the lawyer. Naturally, F. Lee Bailey's time and attention are worth more than attorney who is just starting out in practice. The factors which influence the fee are the amount of work required and the complexity of the situation. For example, questions the attorney will probably ask will be the amount and type of property involved, whether custody of children is disputed, and whether the divorce is contested. Some lawyers charge on a contingency basis, which means they get paid a percentage of the final settlement. You should find out which basis the lawyer uses and the method by which payments are to be made before you begin. Most lawyers expect a "retainer," which is an amount of money paid before he accepts the case. This is particularly common in divorces where experi ence has shown that parties who enter divorce action in the heat of anger may later cool and call the whole thing off, leaving the lawyer high and dry. The couple who has made up after a lover's quarrel isn't very interested in ever seeing the attorney again, let alone paying those bills!

You should find out if there will be extra charges, such as long distance phone calls, court appearances, etc. Will the lawyer accept installment payments? If so, when are the payments due? In a divorce you also need to know whether your husband can be expected to pay the fees, if there will be a split, or whether you will be personally responsible. Also, many attorneys will ask you to sign a fee agreement at the outset of their representation. If the attorney you interview uses a fee agreement, ask him to review it with you. Make sure you understand the entire agreement.

Remember, as you get the answers to these questions, it is most important that you jot them down. You may be surprised at how differently each attorney answers them. One attorney may think you have a cut-and-dried custody situation, another may be more guarded in her assessments. One may seem optimistic about your property settlement, another may express doubts. You need to weigh the opinion of each lawyer carefully. You also need to consider your own feelings about each lawyer in light of how you may feel about your situation in general. Granted, you may be very resentful that you are in a situation which requires an attorney. Now that this has happened, can you work with this individual?

Sometimes, the *situation* will dictate the caliber of lawyer which you hire. If your divorce is being hotly contested, if there is a lot of property involved, if your husband has hired a top-notch lawyer, you will need a different kind of lawyer than a woman who has already reached an agreement with her husband and anticipates very little difficulty in untying the legal knot.

Earlier in this chapter, we emphasized the importance of having a good rapport with your attorney. Your feelings about an attorney are just as important as your judgement of his expertise. You will work closely with this person for a long time. Does he make an effort to help you feel at ease? Is he empathetic? Does he seem genuinely understanding about the human aspects of your situation? Does he appear to give you his full attention or is he being interrupted by secretaries and phone calls? Does his office seem to be efficient and well run or is his desk a mountain of confused files, papers and letters? Is his secretary pleasant or did you have the impression she is about to have a nervous breakdown? Some excellent lawyers *do* look like and live in the disorganized manner in which they are frequently depicted in TV series but, in general, orderly and efficient surroundings are a good clue as to how your case will be handled.

We cannot overemphasize the need for good communication. Talking to a lawyer is very much like talking to a doctor. Neither professional can help you very much unless you candidly tell them everything they need to know. Some things you may need to discuss with your lawyer are very personal and it would be quite natural for you to experience some embarrassment. This is why finding the right lawyer will help. Remember, a lawyer is a professional and is ethically bound to keep your communication in the strictest confidence. Even if you do not choose to retain a particular lawyer, he or she cannot go down and discuss your situation at the cocktail lounge after you leave.

We have just said certain communication may cause you a feeling of embarrassment in discussions about sex, religion and politics. But we believe the most embarrassing subject of all may be *money*. After you have interviewed several attorneys and found the one you want to represent you, be sure to get any fee agreement in writing. If you feel embarrassed even imagining yourself asking for such an agreement, you are another case underlining the truth. Money is the most embarrassing subject of all!

Once you have gone through all this effort to hire the right attorney for you, the progress of your divorce or probate may almost seem anticlimactic. You may wish to evaluate the work your lawyer is doing. Here are some key questions. Does she return your phone calls? Does she send you memos of progress? Do you receive accurate monthly statements of your account? In other words, does she seem to be paying an appropriate amount of attention to your case? Try to be realistic and fair about this. If you husband repeatedly threatens you with bodily harm or continually harasses you and your children, you have a right to call your attorney at any hour of the day or night. On the other hand, if you are constantly calling your attorney at the drop of a hat because you have nothing else to do, that doesn't mean *she* has nothing else to do. If you are calling your lawyer just to get attention, you know it and she knows it, too. If you are being a pest, you aren't doing your case any good. The best thing to do is to exercise self-discipline and make a note when you think of a question you want to ask your attorney. Save that question and any others for a certain time on a certain day of the week that you will allow yourself to call. Remember that the legal proceeding may be the biggest thing in your life but it is not the biggest thing in your attorney's life. Emotionally distraught clients who are unable to separate the legal and financial concerns from the terrible grief they are experiencing are no help to their attorney.

Inherent in the attorney-client relationship is the protected right of the client to transfer his or her case to another attorney. If, after all efforts to resolve your differences, you are completely at odds with your attorney, you may switch to another, and it is a right which will be scrupulously protected by the courts. Before announcing your decision, however, you should ask for a statement of fees incurred to date. This is because there may be a temptation on the part of the attorney you dismiss to feel disgruntled and to raise your fees if you ask for a billing *after* you dismiss him.

If you seek the counsel of a new and different attorney, the two lawyers will usually cooperate to effectuate a smooth transition of your case. They will fully review the issues and problems of your case as well as the vested fees of the first attorney.

What happens if the first attorney refuses to gracefully step aside? If this unusual but conceivable event occurs, your new choice of counsel will have to file an appropriate motion in court to have the other attorney removed. But because the court will be careful to protect the earned fees of your first attorney, it is best to avoid this.

There is another reason for replacing an attorney, too. Just like in the movies and soap operas, real lawyers fall in love with real clients. If you find yourself in this position, go ahead and play the role, it may be wonderfully satisfying to find yourself in love again. *But,* this is no longer the person to impartially represent you in a court of law. Switch lawyers and enjoy the romance, if you wish.

If, despite all our suggestions, you find yourself in serious disagreement with your attorney over a fee or some aspect of your case and you cannot seem to resolve it on your own, you may find recourse through your local Bar Association. Most Bar Associations have a client relations committee to help settle disputes between attorneys and clients.

While we will discuss this in greater detail later, let us give you a strong word of caution. You will encounter many legal documents in divorce and probate proceedings. Make sure you understand every single thing you sign. If necessary, you may ask for a written statement explaining the document in terms you can understand. This is your right. This is your responsibility. This is an opportunity to exercise your assertiveness. And, it can certainly prevent some rude awakenings in your future!

Finally, we have some suggestions for the inquisitive and determined. You are certainly encouraged to delve into all the codes and statutes that are suddenly of interest to you. While it would be foolhardy to pretend that such reading will put you into a position to handle your own case, it *will* ease your mind and help you to understand and cooperate with your attorney.

Getting out gracefully

On your wedding day you certainly had no idea that your marriage would end in divorce. You are not alone if you feel your dreams and illusions are shattered. We all cling to fantasies that love is forever and the romance will never die.

Every woman is unique and every marriage is unique. Some marriages are full of fights and crises. Dishes and furniture are thrown. Stormy scenes are followed by equally turbulent reconciliations. One of you packs up and moves out so routinely that the other knows this "end" will not be the end at all.

In some marriages, the physical warfare is not apparent. Instead, a tense and hostile war of nerves is being waged. There are days of frozen silences and hateful stares. You find countless ways of getting back at each other without allowing the friction to break out into an open fight.

Then there are some marriages where the problem is more subtle but nonetheless very real. Companionship has reached the point of intolerable boredom. The romance has long since died. One day you suddenly realize that to continue in the rut would be suicide. You want a real relationship with a real human being, not a psychological clone.

Some marriages are very enduring. They are loving, supportive, creative commitments until suddenly one day something goes wrong. There are so many pressures pushing down on even the best of matches. Problems in communication,

money anxiety, alcohol, child rearing, sex, "male meno-
pause" or "the women's movement" are just some of the factors contributing to our dramatic rise in divorces.

So now the divorce is happening to you. You may have init-
iated it yourself after a long period of soul searching and
heartbreaking attempts to patch things up. You may, on the
other hand, be the "victim." Your husband is the one who
wants out, perhaps for another woman. Whatever your marriage was like, whether or not you're the one who wants it to
end, at times it will be nearly impossible for you to believe
this is really happening to you.

Divorce is a legal proceeding. It will also be a very stressful
emotional experience for you. You may feel as much trauma
as if someone close to you had died. Social scientists agree
that the transition of divorce ranks second in trauma only to
the experience of widowhood. You may even feel at times
that being a widow would be more merciful. At least death
would save you from the painful ambivalence you are experiencing. Instead, you will have to deal with this man, the one
in your shattered romantic dreams, again and again.

The emotional trauma of divorce cannot be overempha-
sized. On the average, it takes a woman three to five years to
fully "recover." While this chapter deals with the legal and
financial technicalities, we urge you to reread the chapter on
grief as the feelings of hurt and disappointment well up inside
you.

Community organizations and even churches are finally
becoming sensitive to the adjustment problems of the woman
going through a divorce. Times are changing but not fast
enough. You may find yourself on the defensive with your
parents, ex-in-laws, older relatives or judgmental and rigid
peers. If you have children, they too will put pressures on you
because of the losses they are experiencing. You are bound to
discover that between your own grief and the pressures of
those around you, this divorce is going to mean things will
never again be the way they were. What we will do in this
chapter is prepare you to get through your divorce so that

someday in the future, even though things will still be different, they will be better than you are able to anticipate at this
time.

We have talked previously about choosing an attorney.
Perhaps you are beginning the task of finding a good lawyer.
Possibly you have already talked to more than one by telephone. Now you are ready for the initial interview. It isn't
just good lawyers who get good results, but good clients as
well.

Women who are prepared, realistic, organized and stable
when they begin divorce proceedings start out better and
consequently end up better. Maybe you laughed when you
read that sentence. How can you possibly be prepared, realistic, organized and stable when your whole life is falling
apart? It's like trying to carry on your half of that pleasant
little conversation with the dentist while he's got a drill, an
aspirator, and four fingers in your mouth. Impossible, right?
Wrong! Somewhere, underneath all that hurt, confusion, bitterness, anger and fear is the confident, optimistic woman
you once were, or want to be, the "real you." Have some
faith in the real you!

"Getting it together" after a divorce is a long, uphill journey. Like the old saying, it begins with a single step. You can
put your best foot forward by believing in yourself. If you *act*
prepared, realistic, organized and stable, pretty soon you will
be prepared, realistic, organized and stable.

One way to begin is to know what you want to get out of
your divorce. Your attorney can't tell you what you want.
She can only tell you how to get what you want, if it is realistic. At this point you must begin to carve out your own new
life.

For women whose only goal has been devotion to husband
and children, this may be difficult. You're used to having a
hand in setting goals and making decisions, but probably you
have found yourself taking second place to your husband's
career or your children's needs. Try to expand your thinking,
a little bit at a time. What are some of those things you al-

27

ways said you wanted to do? Live in the city instead of the suburbs? Learn to drive? Make pottery instead of puff pastries? Have a real career instead of just a job? Spend more, or less, time with your children?

Try looking at yourself in some new roles. As your desires for the future take shape, you will find it easier to make many of the decisions you need to make during a divorce proceeding.

For example, let's suppose you are a woman who is a college graduate, married for ten years, with three children. You have been working for the past five years as a real estate broker. You and your husband have a four bedroom home in the suburbs, a sailboat, some bonds and a good sized savings account.

You may decide you want to quit your job, sell your house, move to a nearby city, and enroll in law school.

Or, you may decide that you like your job. It gives you ample income and the time you need to spend with your children. You feel your children have suffered in the divorce and need special counseling. You also feel it is important for their stability that they remain in familiar surroundings.

Then again, you may decide that suburban living is something you put up with for your husband's career. You'd feel much better moving back to Iowa, where your folks live. You know you can support yourself comfortably there and you want your kids to grow up in a small town like you did.

In each of these alternatives, you would want alimony, division of property, child support and child custody arrangements to be structured very differently to meet your specific goals.

We're not saying that goals like these are always obtainable. They may or may not be realistic. Your husband may have equally strong and conflicting goals, particularly when children are involved. What we are saying is that if you know what you want, you have a much better chance of getting it.

An experienced lawyer understands that this is perhaps the worst time in your life. She has come to terms with the fact that happy people do not walk into her office. Her satisfaction comes from seeing her clients walk out in better shape than when they walked in. Your job is to know what you want and to work with your attorney in a prepared, organized and realistic fashion to obtain your specific goals.

Who, What, When and Where?

Getting organized means rounding up lots of information for your attorney. You will need a complete list of your assets and liabilities as well as the monthly income and living expenses of both you and your husband. You probably don't feel like doing this. It's like having the doorbell ring when you're putting out a fire in your kitchen!

Your head is exploding with other questions and concerns. "My husband is having an affair. What should I do about it?" "My husband is abusing our children. How can I keep him away from them?" "My husband knows I'm having an affair and he's threatening divorce himself." "My husband knows I want a divorce and he won't give me any money to live on."

Your need for answers is urgent. But until your attorney knows specifically what your situation is, she can only give general advice. This isn't very helpful. You want advice tailored to your unique situation. You want a carefully devised plan of action. This is only possible when your attorney has details to work from. The sooner you can provide these, the better. This way you will insure that the plans and strategy devised at your initial session with your attorney will be more realistic. The assessment of any legal and factual problems will be more complete. You will also prevent the need to change goals or strategies later on.

Our chapter entitled "Putting Your Financial House in Order" will give you lots of information about assets and liabilities and help in getting your monthly income and living expenses pinned down. Most attorneys have forms for you to fill out which will also help organize the information. You

Alone

will need to provide statistical information about your marriage, your husband, your children and yourself. Sometimes this information is obtained by use of a questionnaire. A sample questionnaire is included at the end of this chapter to give you an indication of what to expect.

At the initial interview, bring as many documents as you conveniently can. Here are examples of the kinds of documents that your attorney would like to see:

RECENT INCOME TAX RETURNS	RECENT APPRAISALS
THREE YEARS	LOAN APPLICATIONS
PAYCHECK STUBS	EMPLOYMENT AGREEMENTS
PASSBOOKS	PENSION AND PROFIT
STOCK CERTIFICATES	SHARING PLANS
BONDS	INSURANCE POLICIES
DEEDS	BUDGET BOOKS

The more of this kind of information you can bring to an initial interview, the better the meeting, and the more accurate the assessment and advice you will get.

You may not be able to get your hands on very much information before your initial interview. If your husband doesn't know you are consulting an attorney, too much fooling around in the files at home or at work will raise suspicions! If your husband knows but is uncooperative, sometimes the only way to get information is through legal process. We will talk more about this later. You should discuss these kinds of problems with your attorney on the telephone at the time you set up the initial appointment.

For most family law practitioners, many portions of the initial interview are standard. The same basic information is required from the client in all cases. Similarly, many of the questions that you will ask have been asked before. Nonetheless the lawyer's advice and approach can vary significantly depending on your attitude, goals, stability, age and economic circumstances. Providing your lawyer with good solid information by honest and truthful answers to the questions she

30

asks is the best way to build a good solid case. This guarantees that your lawyer's approach to your divorce is tailored for you.

Why Me?

Remember, you can't expect your attorney to function as a marriage or psychological counselor. She is not trained to do this and her hourly rates, on the average, are higher than those in the counseling professions. On the other hand, your attorney does need to know if emotional problems exist and, if so, how severe they are.

One of the most common "emotional" problems is not wanting the divorce in the first place. If you feel this way, tell your lawyer. One of her strategies can be delay. She may also be able to give you some advice on family and marriage counseling.

Unfortunately, it takes two people to get married but often only one to get a divorce. Especially in "no fault" states, if your husband wants the divorce, he will usually get it. On the other hand, if you believe time is an ally, some time can be bought for you in the legal process. Even if this does not avert the inevitable, it may allow you vital psychological adjustment time.

In "fault" states with contested divorces, it is occasionally possible for you to defeat a divorce requested by your husband. However, it is the opinion of many lawyers practicing in this area that the person who succeeds in preventing a divorce has not really gained anything. All you have is the temporary perpetuation of an unhappy and progressively unhappier situation.

Whose Fault Is No Fault?

The national trend is toward "no fault" divorce. A no-fault divorce means that the questions of who wants the divorce and why are no longer argued in court. This simply means that neither you nor your husband needs to allege or prove specific reasons for a divorce. For example, it doesn't matter who is "mistreating" who, which one of you is having an affair, or which one of you is responsible or irresponsible. All that matters is that one of you wants a divorce and says there are "irreconcilable differences."

This also means the relative "guilt" or "innocence" of you or your husband is not used to divide property or provide for support. Some states have a combination of divorce laws. Such states permit a no-fault divorce after a period of separation, but otherwise require a fault divorce.

You may begin to wonder why the state is so concerned about your marriage and divorce anyway. After all, you always thought it was a private thing between you and your husband. Why should two adults have to give any reasons to anybody for something they want to do?

The state has an interest in promoting families and the stability they provide. For this reason, it has a corresponding interest in preventing divorce. Like it or not, in all of the fifty states, a divorce can only be obtained with the state's "permission." The rules of pleading and procedure which govern divorce are, in reality, the manner in which people seek the state's permission.

Now we will take a look at these rules of pleading and procedure, the divorce process itself.

The First Step Is Filing

The actual legal process of divorce begins with the filing of a document by either your husband or yourself. The document is a *petition* or a *complaint* requesting a divorce. Your attorney files it for you with the court. This document will usually contain some statistical information about you, your husband and the marriage. Generally, it will include the reason that a divorce is being requested and, perhaps, information about the property of the marriage, the debts of the marriage and the children. Courts usually charge a fee to process these documents. This is sometimes referred to as a filing fee. For purposes of clarity, we will refer to the initial pleading as a petition.

The next logical step is to let the other spouse know that a divorce is being sought. After the petition has been filed, the court issues a *summons*, which must be served on the *defendant (respondent)*. In most cases, both you and your husband will know the divorce is pending. You may decide together which one of you is going to file the petition and which one of you will be the defendant. Service of the summons can be a big surprise but in most cases it is merely a necessary legal procedure and is accomplished in some friendly manner which avoids embarrassment to the defendant. You can arrange to have your husband "served" privately in his office. He can pick the papers up from your attorney. Or you can have them mailed to his attorney's office. Wherever the papers are served, a receipt for them will be acknowledged and the measure of time within which they must be answered will begin. This time varies from state to state.

Temporary Orders for Immediate Needs

Now, remember all those questions you had? Divorces take time. Many cases involve enough economic, emotional or legal complexities to make it impossible to obtain a divorce in a short period of time. Yet, you know there are problems which need immediate attention.

Who gets the children? Who supports them? What about alimony? How do I make the house payments? Who pays for the repairs? Who pays the attorney's retainer? Can I still use my charge cards? He's closing out all our joint accounts and harassing me and the children. How can I stop him?

Problems like these can't wait. Most states have temporary orders available to deal with your immediate needs. The judge is given a limited amount of information, whatever is available at the time. He will then attempt to maintain the "status quo." He wants to preserve order while the larger and more complex and time consuming problems of the divorce are worked out.

At this time you, your husband, your attorneys and the court will decide how much money you will have, temporarily, to live on each month, who stays in the house and who moves, how custody of the children will be handled, and how you and your husband will meet your various financial obligations.

Many of these issues can be agreed upon by you and your husband. Most courts encourage efforts at mutual agreement. After all, you and your husband have more information about your personal and financial status than either of your attorneys or the judge.

If at any time during this period you or your children are harassed by your husband or threatened with violence, contact your attorney immediately. The court will take action to protect your right to safety and privacy.

Assets and Liabilities:
What Are They and Where Do They Go?

After the dust settles on the temporary questions, the emphasis shifts. Everyone begins to focus on the final outcome of the case.

Some of the same problems are dealt with on a permanent level that were determined on a temporary level. And again the court considers support, both child and spousal, custody, attorneys' fees, and costs.

This time the division of the assets and liabilities of the marriage receives most of the attention. You may think of divorce as simply "splitting the sheets," dividing your assets and liabilities, whether fifty-fifty as in no-fault states, or according to some other formula. You may become impatient when your attorney is unable to do this immediately. If you find yourself feeling this way, remember, there are two important preliminary stages in the division of assets and liabilities. These stages are identification and valuation.

If you are not at all sure what you and your husband own, you are not alone. You may be living the life of foreign cars and country clubs only to find out the bank owns all your luxuries or everything is being expensed by your husband's corporation. This could mean a dramatic change in your lifestyle.

On the other hand, perhaps you've been hearing "We can't afford that" all your married life, only to find there are all sorts of investments that your husband put in his own name. That doesn't necessarily mean they are all his.

Difficulties are often encountered in identifying the property of a marriage. Sometimes, your husband has been less than candid about what is owned and what is owed. In other cases, there are legal questions about the ownership and nature of the property. For instance, is it community or separate property? In some states, property which is inherited or received as a gift is considered the separate property of the spouse receiving it. Other problems include joint tenancy interests held with someone other than the spouse, problems created by people who have been married more than once, and prenuptial agreements that may contain ambiguities. There are also those problems that result from the commingling of property that may once have been separate property with community property.

In community property states, it is easier to determine who owns what, especially if the marriage was long. The community property states are California, Arizona, Nevada, Texas, Washington, Idaho, New Mexico and Louisiana. If you live in one of these states, all of the property acquired during your marriage, except by gift or inheritance, is considered to be community property.

If you live in a non-community property state, ownership is often determined by the manner in which title is held. This makes the identification of commingled property a more difficult task.

If your husband has always been very secretive about the marriage property, you may wonder how you will ever get

Alone

him to own up to things now. Be assured this is not the first time such a marriage has ended in divorce. The court provides ways of dealing with the situation.

To insure that the information needed will be forthcoming and that the parties will be reasonably candid with each other, attorneys are permitted to conduct what is euphemistically called "discovery." There are several methods of discovery. The most commonly used is the *deposition.* A deposition is usually taken in an informal setting, often a lawyer's office. It involves a question and answer process which takes place before a court reporter, you and your husband, and your attorneys. Your attorney will ask questions of your husband or a witness. Your attorney's questions and the answers are taken down verbatim by the court reporter. The person being "deposed" is under oath to tell the truth. A deposition may be used not only to secure information from husband or wife but also from third persons like employers.

Your attorney can also use *subpoenas* and *interrogatories.* Subpoenas are court orders demanding the production of certain documents or files. Interrogatories are similar to depositions except they are *written* questions and answers. The advantage of interrogatories is that the person answering must make an effort to locate information necessary for a complete answer. In a deposition, "I don't know" and "I can't remember" are acceptable answers. In interrogatories, they are not.

After all your assets and liabilities have been identified through information you provide or by any of the discovery procedures, there may still be problems in the area of valuation. Generally speaking, the less *unique* an asset, the easier it is to value. Cash is the least unique asset of all, and, therefore, the easiest to value. Stocks which are traded on an exchange are also easy to value. As assets become more unique, such as real property, businesses, and art works, they become more difficult to value. It is often necessary to enlist the help of accountants, appraisers and other experts. While on a mathematical level it's easy enough to divide two into a given number to effect an equal division, you can see that coming

36

up with the given number is quite a job. Only after all your assets and liabilities have been identified and valued, can your attorney begin to assist you in the actual division. Even then, you need to be in touch with the gap between monetary value and sentimental value.

While you are not at all delighted to be following the surge of recent divorces, you will reap some benefits because others have pioneered this territory before you. The shifting legal emphasis toward the location, valuation and division of property has led to some sophisticated business and tax concepts in the field of divorce. You are familiar with the obvious types of property such as cash, real estate, stocks and bonds, but a good lawyer can assist in helping you to understand even more. Your attorney may favorably influence your final position by discovering cash value or death benefits of life insurance policies, residual contract rights, patents and copyrights, notes receivable, good will, potential recoveries in law suits, and other contract rights.

Which Will It Be: Settlement or Trial?

Once the discovery and valuation phase is complete, you and your attorney can begin an informed discussion of what you specifically want in the way of a permanent resolution or settlement. There are only two ways for you and your husband to reach an ultimate resolution: by yourselves with your attorneys' help (settlement) or with the judge's help (trial).

Settlements offer greater latitude and fewer risks than having a case tried by a judge. You and your husband, in trying to settle, consider not only the economic and monetary value of certain items but their importance to each other as well. You can use intimate knowledge of each other to better assess and predict the future. This means more realistic decisions in the present.

If the matter goes to trial, you and your husband are less likely to get a solution tailor-made to your situation and your goals.

First of all, the judge has very little time in which to hear and decide a case. Although some trials last a few weeks, many last only a few hours.

Secondly, the judge has much less knowledge, no matter how well the case is presented, about who you and your husband are, what you own, and what you want, than you do.

Thirdly, there are certain aspects of a division, like tax consequences, that a judge may be unable, by law, to consider.

Fourthly, judges are human and may have certain prejudices about the behavior of husbands and wives, alimony, custody, or other aspects of a case. As a rule judges are conscientious, hardworking people who try to be fair. Yet a judge can never be as aware in your own case as you are. There is an element of risk every time a case is submitted to a third party for a decision.

Finally, going to trial can also breed lasting bitterness. You may be able to avoid this by settling.

The process of trying to settle without a trial is referred to as *negotiation*. Negotiation is more or less successful in approximately eighty percent of the domestic cases in which it is used.

It is important that you keep the lines of communication open with your husband while you are negotiating. This may seem like a lot to ask, but it's well worth the trouble.

Your attorney can be most helpful by suggesting creative solutions. Many women, especially those untrained or unused to the business world, are unaware of the many ways in which a property division can be accomplished. Beyond the obvious half-for-you and half-for-me division in kind of money or other property, you can negotiate and settle using promissory notes, tax considerations, support or the lack of support, loans and other financial transactions that are common in the business world. Settlements can be tailor-made to your health, education, financial status, talents, attitudes and goals.

Let's get back to our earlier example where you imagined

yourself as a woman who had been married for ten years, with three children and five years experience as a real estate broker. Suppose you decided to go to law school. You would need cash for tuition, moving and living expenses. On the other hand, you would not need your house and probably wouldn't be very interested in the sailboat. You might also want your husband to have custody of your children. If so, you would not be concerned about child support.

If you decided instead that you enjoyed your job and would keep it but were concerned about counseling for your children and providing them with a stable environment, custody and child support would be extremely important to you. You would also be very concerned about staying in your family home. You might like to have the sailboat, also.

In the third alternative, deciding to move back to Iowa, custody and child support would be extremely important. You would also need cash for relocation expenses and to tide you over until you established yourself as a broker back home. You would obviously not need the family home or the sailboat.

In each of these alternatives, your attorney can give valuable advice to help you meet your goals. When you begin negotiating, the important thing is to know where you want to end up and *what you are willing to give up in order to get there.* A good settlement is usually one in which both you and your husband are less than satisfied with the results. It's "fair" when you both feel you have made some compromises.

The easiest division of property would be to sell all the assets and divide the cash proceeds. This is rarely done because of the economic hardships it would create. There are usually many assets that either cannot or should not be sold and cannot be divided. In cases like this, the asset is awarded to one spouse with an award of another asset to the other spouse to balance the division.

If you and your husband have only one asset, or a single asset which far exceeds the value of all the others combined, such as a house, the division of property becomes difficult. In this case, the person retaining the asset usually agrees to pay the other spouse, either in a lump sum or in installments, the value of that spouse's share. This kind of division can lead to tax problems and requires the advice of an accountant or tax lawyer.

Aside from value, there are other factors to consider in the division of property. One factor is the property's tax basis and the corresponding capital gain that will some day have to be paid when and if it is sold. Other questions to be considered are these: Which property produces income? Which property is appreciating? Which property can be depreciated for tax purposes? Is the property a passive or an active investment? The income produced by a property or, correspondingly, the money required to carry it is also considered in an award of spousal support to one party or the other.

Finally Comes the Judgment

After your case has been settled either out of court or by trial, a written *judgment* (decree) is prepared by your attorney. The written judgment reflects the decisions that have been reached regarding property, spousal and child support and custody. In some states, this judgment is immediately or automatically final; in others there is a waiting period. Generally, in all states there is some waiting period involved in obtaining a divorce; sometimes before the petition can be filed, sometimes between the date of filing and judgment, sometimes between one or more judgments. This waiting period exists because of the state's historical interest in the preservation of marriage as a stable social institution.

Your Day in Court

Even when you and your husband have settled issues of property, custody and support, it is still usually necessary for one of you, at least, to make a court appearance to "testify to the grounds" for divorce. In no-fault states the court may need to be informed of several things. You may need to testify that there has been an irremediable breakdown of the marriage or that irreconcilable differences have arisen between you and your husband. You may need to show that the residency requirements for obtaining a divorce are met.

In fault states, you or your husband must prove to the court the existence of one of the specific grounds your state recognizes for granting a divorce. The most common grounds are adultery, desertion, and some form of mental or physical cruelty. If these grounds seem humdrum, a sampling of the laws of the fifty states reveals some even more unusual grounds, such as impotency, conviction of a felony with a death sentence, public defamation, an attempt on the life of the other spouse, nonsupport, intemperance, and confinement to a mental hospital for three years with no probability of recovery.

The trend in divorce law is definitely toward no–fault divorce. There are a couple of sound reasons for this. It is often time consuming, expensive, unfair and ultimately embittering, to prove some of the more technical and detailed grounds for divorce mentioned above. Also, it may be argued that property division and support should bear little relation to the relative guilt or innocence of the parties since it costs no less to eat when one is guilty than when one is innocent. This trend means that more emphasis is placed on division of property and awarding of support and your lawyer's primary efforts will be expended in this regard. The emotional bomb that was once present in the divorce courtroom and popularly reproduced for television is being defused. At the least, those scenes are now removed from the courtroom arena. Whether it is less dramatic and more humane, or not, parties are now urged to view their divorce from an economic standpoint.

The Alimony Money

For almost all women going through a divorce, perhaps the touchiest subject, with the exception of custody, is alimony.

To most lawyers, it is just money and to most clients, it is much, much more. It is perhaps the hardest single area to settle in domestic cases and the one where it is hardest for the lawyer to convince her client of what is a fair and reasonable result.

Alimony is no longer the prerogative of wives. It may surprise you to learn that in thirty-two of the fifty states, alimony can be awarded to the husband! Laws that provide for alimony on the basis of sex are regularly being struck down by the US Supreme Court as a denial of equal protection. Within a few years, men, upon showing of need, should be able to get alimony in all fifty states.

The women's movement has emphasized that work within the home is "real work." At cocktail parties, women who went straight from their parents' home to their husband's are now much more likely to say, "I have never worked *outside the home*." The purpose of alimony is neither punishment nor retroactive payment for services already rendered. The purpose of alimony is to achieve a balance of economic necessities and realities during the period of separation and divorce. Alimony exists to help the spouse who has worked within the home but out of the job market. By paying alimony, the spouse who worked outside the home assists the other to become employable and self-sufficient rather than shifting that burden to the government and to the welfare rolls.

In all states the most important considerations in awarding alimony are the need of one spouse for it and the ability of the other spouse to pay it. All other factors taken into consideration are secondary. In determining needs, courts do consider the source and amount of income of the recipient spouse, the health, education, age and employability of both spouses, the expenses of both spouses, the lifestyle of the parties and the length of the marriage. In states where there is fault divorce, the degree of fault is also involved in the awarding of alimony.

An important fact about alimony is that, unlike child support, it is fully taxable to the spouse receiving it and fully deductible to the spouse paying it. This means if you receive alimony you will pay tax on it as ordinary income. If your husband is in the fifty percent tax bracket, the cost of alimony to him is fifty cents on the dollar. Putting it another way, for every dollar he earns, half would go to the federal government anyway. So the out-of-pocket amount he pays is really only fifty cents.

If your husband is in a high tax bracket, alimony can be almost a license to steal. It is often used as a disguise for property division and child support payments. Alimony, once awarded, is rarely modified upward.

If your husband is in a high tax bracket, he will prefer to pay alimony rather than lump sum settlements or child support because of the tax advantages to him. Since this is something he wants, it can be a good negotiating tool for you. The best way to avoid being taken advantage of in the alimony game is to get yourself a smart lawyer. With good professional advice, you can use alimony to your own advantage as a negotiating tool.

Don't Forget the Children

Child support is probably the most predictable result of any divorce proceeding involving children. It is also the most psychologically acceptable settlement to both parents. In most states, the obligation to support children financially falls on both parents. In those states where child support falls first on the father, the laws are being successfully challenged on appeal as a denial of equal protection. Many courts have guidelines for determining the cost of raising a child in a particular location and will award child support on that basis. Sometimes, however, there are particular facts making it unusually expensive to raise a given child, such as handicaps or unusual talents. Such issues always should be brought up for court consideration.

Support is awarded until a child reaches the age of eighteen or twenty-one, depending on the age of majority in a given state. In most states, this support cannot be waived by either parent. The money received is tax free to the custodial parent and therefore is a particularly important negotiating tool for the custodial parent.

If you are negotiating a settlement and intend to have custody of your children, you should consider other provisions besides basic support for your children's future security. You will want to think about such things as college education, private school, life insurance protection, medical and dental expenses such as orthodontic and psychiatric care, and anything else you think would be fair considering your own and your husband's financial situation and your mutual expectations for your children.

In addition, you should negotiate child support payments that increase automatically as your children grow older and the cost of living increases. While it is possible to take your husband back to court at a later time to increase his child support payments, this in itself is a costly procedure. You will save time and money by building in automatic increases at the time you negotiate your divorce settlement.

The Child Support Drawback

Unfortunately, the discussion of child support must be concluded with some bad news. Payments under most support orders are discontinued somewhere between commencement of and five years after the award is made. This area of enforcement, concerning spousal and child support, is perhaps the most dismal area of divorce law. For both child and spousal support, normal methods of enforcing a judgment such as execution on assets and garnishment of wages are available. In many cases, however, enforcing the judgment will cost you as much or more than you'd be getting if your husband paid in the first place. Naturally, this leaves you in a real dilemma.

You may also bring a criminal contempt proceeding to try to enforce payment. In a contempt case, the result of nonpayment is that your husband will be jailed. This normally does not result in payment unless there is money available. Neither spousal nor child support payments are discharged in bankruptcy and the statutes of limitation applicable to the collection of both are usually lengthy.

It's not a pretty picture. But you and your children may unfortunately find yourselves painted into it. At least with child support, great strides have been made by the federal government in opening files to local law enforcement agencies to assist in locating defaulting parents. The Department of Health, Education and Welfare maintains a parent locator service and the federal government has permitted garnishments of federal employees' wages for child support. Many district attorneys, under the Uniform Reciprocal Enforcement of Support Act, maintain family support divisions which assist in locating defaulting parents and enforcing payment.

The Touchy Question of Custody

No matter how long or difficult a division of property and resolution of support can be, they pale by comparison to a proceeding involving custody of minor children. Litigation over custody is emotional and frightening and compromises are often not possible. Many experts feel the child or children always lose a custody battle no matter which parent "wins."

There are two types of custody. One is *legal* custody which involves the right to make decisions about the child's welfare, education, religious training and medical treatment. There is also *physical* custody which involves the day-to-day care of the child. Most often, the same parent has legal and physical custody.

A more recent innovation in this area has been the use of *joint* custody. You can have either *joint legal custody, joint physical custody* or *joint legal and physical custody*. In some cases, custody actually is joint in the sense that both parents do spend fifty percent of the child's available time with the child. This is usually possible when parents live near enough to each other that the child can continue to maintain friendships and attend the same school throughout the year. Joint custody is workable only when the parents have a very amicable divorce. If there is hostility, your inability to deal with each other will only continue in the joint custody arrangement.

Parents and the courts have also been known to separate children when there is more than one in a family. One child lives with the mother and the other resides with the father. This is generally a disfavored method of custody. In determining the placement of a child, most courts consider the desires of the child if he or she is of sufficient age, usually around the age of fourteen, and possesses the capability to express a preference.

Actually, determination of custody involves very little law. Simply, the court is bound to make an award that is in the "best interests of the child." That determination is usually a question of fact rather than one of law. Many states still retain a statutory preference for the mother, especially when the children are young, but like other laws indicating a sexual basis, these too are being changed. Nonetheless, it is easier to legislate new laws than attitudes. Many judges still retain a psychological preference for the mother in custody cases. In states having a statutory preference for the mother, it is necessary to prove that she is unfit before custody can be awarded to the father. In states having no statutory preference, it is not necessary to prove either parent unfit unless an award of custody is being made to a nonparent.

Even in no-fault states, fault enters the picture in a custody battle. The court may consider any information that is relevant in determining the abilities of either parent to provide for the child. In making a determination, the court looks to as much objective evidence as it can find, since the parties themselves are too emotionally involved. Sometimes if one listens to the conflicting testimony in a custody case, it is hard to believe that these people are talking about the same children, the same family, and the same environment.

The attorneys and the parties must provide the court with information about the children's school, medical history, outside activities, friends and their parents. Such information demonstrates much more objectively how the children are doing than the testimony of either parent. The court also considers the length of time that a child has lived in a stable and satisfactory environment and the importance of maintaining that continuity. This is considered along with the parents' ability to demonstrate love and affection toward the child, to provide food, clothing and medical care and to promote goals and philosophies of both parents.

Once an award of custody is made, it is subject to the court's continuing jurisdiction to modify it if the circumstances warrant such a modification. Usually the parent who seeks a change of custody must show that circumstances in the child's environment have changed to such a degree that the present custody award is no longer in the child's best interest. Many times in either an original custody proceeding or a modification proceeding, the court will appoint an independent person from a local social welfare agency to investigate the home situations and report back to the court.

The End of the Journey

We have attempted to shed some light on the bewildering realm of divorce. You may have taken this tour out of idle curiosity or desperate personal need. Remember, if you are in the throes of a divorce, it is important to step back to get a better view.

We have charted out for you the peaks and valleys of the legal procedure. You must examine your feelings of grief and stress and include those in your personal chart.

If you did not start this difficult journey feeling prepared, realistic, organized and stable, maybe you'll be feeling that way by the time your divorce is final. It's a landmark on your road to recovery. Stop and look around. Everything is different. We hope it is better.

Alone

Look back where you've come from. Look where you're going. The rest of the journey is yours alone. You will chart it yourself, with your new skills, your new confidence, and your new dreams and goals.

Sample

DOMESTIC RELATIONS QUESTIONNAIRE

This questionnaire is designed to obtain information which we require to evaluate your case, to advise you and prepare necessary pleadings. Please be as complete and accurate as possible.

PART A—FACTUAL INFORMATION
Personal Data—Husband

1. His name: _____
         (First)   (Middle)   (Last)

2. Age:_____.

3. Present Address: _____
               (Street and Number)

               _____
         (City)   (County)   (State)

4. Home Phone Number:_____

5. Length of stay in state: _____years.

6. Birthplace: _____
       (State or Foreign Country)

7. Social security number: _____

8. Present or last occupation:_____

9. Employer: _____

10. Business address: _____
             (Street and Number)

            _____
          (City)   (State)

11. Business Phone Number: _____
Personal Data—Wife

12. Maiden Name: _____
       (First) (Middle) (Maiden Name)

13. If there is to be a dissolution of the marriage, would the wife prefer that her maiden name be restored?_____

(Yes/No)

14. Age:_____

15. Present Address: _____

(Street and Number)

_____

(City)   (County)   (State)

16. Home Phone Number:_____

17. Length of stay in state: _____years.

18. Birthplace: _____

(State or Foreign Country)

19. Social security number: _____

20. Present or last occupation: _____

21. Employer: _____

22. Business address: _____

(Street and Number)

_____

(City)   (State)

23. Business Phone Number: _____

PART B—MARRIAGE/SEPARATION DATA

24. Place of Marriage: _____

(City or Town)   (County)   (State)

25. Date of Marriage: _____

26. Date of Separation:_____

27. Your residence at time of separation: _____

(City or Town)

_____

(County)   (State)

PART C—LIVING CHILDREN OF THIS MARRIAGE

28.

First Name & Middle Initial	Place of Birth (State or Foreign Country)	Date of Birth	Age	Sex

Alone

29. Minor Children's Residence for Last Five Years and With Whom Resided:

Period of Time (Mo. & Yr.)	Address (City & State)	Person(s) Resided With (Include Relationship to Child)

PART D—ASSETS

_____
_____
_____
_____

PART E—LIABILITIES

_____
_____
_____
_____

What every woman should know

This chapter is directed to those of you who have "lost" your husbands. You may be telling people he has "passed on." Euphemisms abound in the English language, particularly, it seems, among women. We do not "sweat," we "glisten" or "glow." We do not go to the "bathroom," we go to the "powder room," or, worse, the "little girl's room." Euphemisms help us over our natural embarrassment about certain things in our lives. But they also hinder effective communication. If you doubt this, next time someone tells you they have an "upset stomach" or they have finally "become involved" with a certain man, ask them, "Exactly what do you mean by that?" The results can be very amusing and a real lesson in communication.

In this chapter we will be talking about the probate process, taxes, and benefits to which you may be entitled as a result of your husband's death.

Terminal illnesses, particularly cancer, death and dying are embarrassing things to talk about for many people. You already know this if you are a widow or if you are realistically preparing for widowhood. You know that embarrassment has even caused some of your friends to avoid you and your "problem" altogether.

If we seem brusque or callous at any time in this chapter, it is not that we are insensitive. We know, from working closely with widows for many years, the very real pain you are going through. We also know how strong you are. Maybe we believe in your strength even more than you do right now. The "Widowed to Widowed One Year Recovery Guarantee" you'll find at the end of this chapter is based on firsthand experience. It really works.

Let's communicate clearly. In this chapter, we need to talk about what happens when your husband is dead. We recognize the hopes, dreams, love, anger, frustration, rage and sorrow, the full range of emotions, that you have associated with your husband's living body and now must grieve. When we talk about "the remains" or "the decedent" or "the deceased," we are simply using words we're comfortable with.

Other societies have found perhaps better ways of dealing with death than ours. In America, however, you will be expected to follow certain rituals of grieving. Usually this includes a burial ceremony of some sort. Then you'll have a very private period of intense mourning where you will be supported by a small group of extremely solicitous close friends and relatives. This period can be very short or last for many months. Gradually you will be expected to resume a normal life. One way of looking at the things you will have to handle financially and legally is that this will help you resume your normal role in society. Even if you feel like it, you can't just withdraw. There are many things you have to take care of.

Some deaths occur suddenly while others follow long illnesses. Some marriages are short and sweet while others are long and bitter. Some couples have made and discussed detailed arrangements on the basis that one would precede the other in death, while many other couples do not even have wills. Some couples do not even share information about the basic financial details of running the household. No matter what the particular circumstances of your own marriage, if you are reading this as a new widow, this is undoubtedly the worst time in your life to have to face the myriad of legal and financial matters that await you. However, you do have work that must be done. Let's begin by looking into some of the benefits to which you may be entitled.

Benefits

The first thing to take care of following your husband's death is, of course, the disposition of his remains. There are many books and pamphlets written on the subjects of funerals, memorial services, cremation, interment, transplants, and donations to science. Generally decisions are made about the disposition of the body soon after the death.

If you are one of the fortunate ones, you know exactly what your husband's wishes were. If you did not discuss them, perhaps he left you written instructions. Sometimes, such requests are included in the will. Obviously, if you are reading this before the decision is to be made, we urge you to get all the information possible and try to make a decision you will neither bemoan yourself nor be criticized for later. You might as well resign yourself to the fact that no matter what you do, someone is bound to find fault with it, even if you only follow the express wishes of your husband!

Contact with the funeral director may be your first opportunity to make poor decisions which will lead to later confusion, or informed decisions which will expedite future business. Generally, the funeral director will give you an opportunity to say how many death certificates you wish to order at approximately two dollars apiece. It is not unusual for a widow to be surprised that one little paper should cost so much. She will ask for only a few copies and then waste many hours of her precious time getting additional ones. It is incredible how many people feel they have a right not only to see, but to keep, an official copy of the death certificate. In some cases, you will be able to show an official death certificate and then submit your own photocopy. In some cases they may even make the copy for you! It is certainly easier to have too many copies of an official death certificate than to attempt to get by with too few. It is not too unusual for a widow to use more than a dozen death certificates in the course of taking care of the business which the death of one's husband requires.

Generally, the funeral director has the proper forms to apply for burial benefits from Social Security and the Veterans Administration. This would be satisfactory if the widow could comprehend what was going on. Unfortunately, the majority of widows come away from the mortuary in confusion. There is a difference between a *one time* death benefit to help pay for the "disposition of the body," Servicemen's Life Insurance, and *ongoing* benefits to which the widow and her children may be entitled. You should always ask for clear written information on *what* benefit has been applied for, *to whom* the check will be issued and *where* it will be mailed. It's also wise to ask approximately *how long* until the check should be expected. Always ask for copies concerning what benefits were applied for on your behalf.

Remember the first chapter about grief? The suggestion we have just made about *writing things down* has to do with two very specific aspects of normal grieving, which are shock and amnesia. Widows, in a normal state of shock, appear to function quite well. You will appear to understand what is being said and you will be expected to remember it. If you actually do remember it all, you will certainly be the exception! Remember, *this is normal.* Help yourself by writing things down in a permanent record. Also, to understand what your husband may have planned or set up financially for you, it may be helpful to turn to the final chapter on Estate Planning which describes in detail various methods employed to efficiently and economically transfer property.

While you are handling these and other matters, you will be dealing with many arms of the huge bureaucracy we call "the government." It is not too unlikely that machinery will grind slowly, red tape will be abundant and there will be confusion and poor communication on the part of the government employees with whom you will deal. It is not unusual to have checks which are sent to you because of your husband's death actually made payable to your husband! You can choose to become very confused and upset at this phenomenon, or you can follow the path of least resistance which is to photo copy the check, deposit it (preferably by mail) and wait to see what happens. If you really are not to have that money, eventually whoever sent it will ask for it back or deduct it from some later payment.

One of the most common misunderstandings in early widowhood in relation to benefits from the federal government is what is a "one time" death benefit such as a "lump sum burial benefit" or Servicemen's Life Insurance and what is to be ongoing support. To add to this confusion is the "retroactive" check which may be an accumulation of the benefit which will be paid on a monthly basis. You are entitled to be paid from the time you apply for some things which is certainly nice to know when you are waiting for months and months for that check which never seems to come.

Here is an example of a retroactive check. A widow who has children under the age of eighteen applies for the money from Social Security to which she is entitled to help her provide for the children since her husband was covered by Social Security. The widow applied two weeks after her husband's death and four months later a substantial check arrives. The months which have elapsed since the death are included in the check. The checks which come regularly thereafter will not be nearly as large.

Some widows hesitate to seek benefits to which they are entitled because they feel it is like seeking welfare. While it is true that certain benefits *are* based on income, it is also true that other benefits are due to all widows and orphans who fall into a certain category regardless of their financial status. Another reason that widows miss out on benefits to which they are entitled is a process we shall call "self editing." The widow decides on her own that she is not entitled to something and "edits herself out of the story" before she has gotten all the facts.

An example that might lend itself to self editing is the "war widow" and "war orphan." At first glance, this would appear only related to those whose husbands or fathers were killed while fighting in a war. Actually, the term applies to any service-connected death. This means that widows and orphans of retired servicemen whose deaths can be directly attributed to a disability caused by their participation in the armed forces, may be entitled to a variety of benefits. These benefits include career counseling and the "G.I. bill" for pursuing educational goals. Too many widows and orphans neglect to claim these vested legal rights because they do not inform themselves of their rights and pursue them. In some cases, this will mean searching out the medical records which show that the cause of death is related to a problem either brought about or which developed while the deceased was on active duty.

The general advice we can offer to all widows is "leave no stone unturned and no question unasked." You have to keep careful records of what you asked, who you asked, and what their answers were. If you are not satisfied, *persevere*. It is not unusual to call the same office on the same day and get three different people with three different answers. For that matter, it's not unheard of to get three different answers from the same person! This is why record keeping and perseverance become paramount.

Try to view things to which you may be entitled as *vested legal rights*, not *welfare*. Perhaps your husband would be alive today if he had not given his all to the government or his company! Now, you are entitled to reap the benefits he worked so hard to provide for you. If this thought does not bolster your sense of courage and perseverance maybe the thought of providing more for your children will motivate you.

Besides money, there may be other benefits to which you are entitled. A lifetime military ID card for you or your children until they finish school may mean significant savings. Free career counseling or tutoring may positively affect the course of your own life or the lives of your children. Perhaps there are free health benefits or continued coverage under a good health plan to consider. While pension funds are already thought of, perhaps there are lodge or union scholarships which were not investigated. It never hurts to ask!

The subject of making insurance claims is covered in our chapter on insurance. We have already urged you to leave no stone unturned or question unasked. An incredible amount of insurance benefits are never claimed. Do not assume that coverage has lapsed or that you are ineligible for benefits. Some insurance policies, such as those with credit purchases or club memberships, can be small but they add up. Even if you cannot locate a particular policy, the insurance company will have a record of it. Money is money, and you are entitled to it.

Tackling "one time" and "ongoing" benefits will be roughly half of your battle as a new widow. The other and probably more difficult half will involve estate administration.

Estate Administration

Simply defined, estate administration is the process of legally transferring or confirming title to property in the estate of a deceased person to those persons who are entitled to receive the property.

Estate administration can be extremely complicated. It may or may not require judicial supervision (probate or surrogate court). It may or may not require the filing of a federal estate tax return or a similar state estate tax return. Other tax returns, at the federal or state level may be required. If judicial supervision is necessary, and you are appointed the estate representative, you will have estate management and administration responsibilities which will vary according to the extent and value of your husband's estate. In some states you will have the option of submitting estate property to the jurisdiction of the probate or surrogate court or petitioning to receive it directly as community property. A choice like this may significantly affect your own liability for your husband's debts.

Estate administration is technically complex and demanding. You'll have to make decisions, interpret and complete forms and file them properly within required deadlines. Even in the best of circumstances, most of us aren't equipped to meet these demands without professional assistance. It is understandable that the grieving process will only compound the difficulty.

In this section we are not attempting to prepare you to administer your husband's estate by yourself. Our best advice is, "Seek competent legal assistance."

Whether you believe your husband's estate is complex or simple, you should consult with an attorney as soon as possible. If you learn in your first visit that probate or other legal actions are not necessary, you will have purchased a lot of emotional security for a relatively small price. If you live in a state which permits you to carry out the probate process without an attorney, and you choose to do so, you may struggle with processes which are routine for an efficient probate attorney's office. We advise against it, but it's your choice. You have to decide at what point savings are overshadowed by confusion, frustration, time, energy and risk.

Our purpose here is to generally describe what happens in estate administration so that it will not be a threatening or disturbing problem or an added burden to you as you work your way through the things you must do.

When you are grieving over the loss of your husband, you generally want to talk about him and remember everything you can. You may wish someone would spend a relaxed afternoon asking such questions as "How did you meet? What was his favorite meal? What special qualities did he possess that endeared him to you?" If such a questioner were to come along, you would be very willing to share every detail.

Unfortunately, when the government comes along, the questions may be just as detailed as "What was his favorite color?" but the queries are of a *very* different nature. It really stretches one's imagination to come up with the complex and detailed questions you will be expected to answer on forms.

To more than one item, you will be inclined to respond, "How the heck should I know?" Restrain yourself! If you can disassociate yourself from the emotional turmoil and pretend it is all a game, you'll be miles ahead.

Whether or not you consult an attor
proceeding, you will need to round up
your husband, your husband'
We'll call this your "data bank." Part
and Social Data and part of it will be (2) *Estate*

Personal and Social Data You Will Need

1. *Personal history of decedent* (date and place of birth, social security number, military service, date of death);

2. *Personal history of surviving spouse* (same as decedent);

3. *Marriage history of decedent* (dates and places of all marriages including explanations of any marriage terminations and including narrative history of all places of residence during marriages);

4. *Employment history of decedent* (names of employers, dates of employment and job descriptions);

5. *Employment history of surviving spouse* (same as decedent);

6. *Names and residence addresses, including dates of birth of all minors, of all heirs of decedent* (nearest relatives including all children, grandchildren, siblings, parents, grandparents. *NOTE:* If none of these relatives is living, then more distant relatives may be required as identified by your attorney);

7. *Names and residence addresses, including dates of birth of all minors, of all beneficiaries named in any existing will.*

Estate Data You Will Need

1. An inventory of all assets owned in whole or in part by decedent at date of death. This inventory should include not only any property titled in decedent's name, but also assets titled jointly with surviving spouse or other parties or titled in the names of parties other than decedent if decedent claimed a proprietary interest in such property. The inventory should

the exact value of assets at date of death and form of

2. An inventory, including narrative history, of all inheritances or gifts received by decedent during his lifetime.

3. An inventory, including narrative history of all separate property of decedent other than listed in 2 above.

4. An inventory of all property acquired by the decedent or by the surviving spouse by their joint or separate labors during marriage.

5. An inventory of all property claimed as the separate property of decedent.

6. An inventory of all property claimed as the separate property of the surviving spouse.

7. A statistical summary of tax returns for the five years preceding date of death. While federal and state income tax returns would certainly be applicable, data regarding other tax returns such as gift tax returns might also be needed.

8. A comprehensive inventory, including narrative history, of all known debts of decedent, of the surviving spouse, and of both of them existing at the date of death.

Whenever possible, your Data Bank should be supported by copies of documents of proof. We can't list them all but the standard documents required in the course of estate administration are as follows:

1. Copies of documents of title to real property and personal property which is titled in written form. Titled personal property includes stocks, bonds, bank accounts, interests in partnerships and leasehold interests.

2. Copies of federal and state income tax returns, and any other tax returns, filed five calendar years before date of death.

3. Certified copies of the death certificate.

4. Copies of documents evidencing purchase transactions of properties held by the deceased at the date of death. For example, escrow papers and contracts regarding purchase of real property, business interests, etc.

Are you slightly aghast? For most people, it's a pain to get organized. Yet the continued frustration you'll face if you can't put your hands on some information or documents far outmeasures the initial effort.

Most people find that a well labeled file box is a great help. If you include in this file box, notes to indicate the location of items which have been removed, you will be miles ahead.

Here's a list of documents and other important papers to help you get started. You may have some additions to this list. You will notice that we have been repetitious. This is to help jog your memory. The organizational secret is being confident you know exactly where these documents and important papers are:

AUTO REGISTRATION

BANK ACCOUNTS

BENEFITS

BIRTH CERTIFICATES AND
   ADOPTION PAPERS

BUSINESS BOOKS &
   AGREEMENTS, INTERESTS

BONDS

CREDIT CARDS, NUMBERS

DEBTS

DEEDS (ABSTRACTS OR OTHER
   EVIDENCE OF TITLE)

DIVORCE PAPERS

EMPLOYMENT & CAREER
   RECORDS

FAMILY RECORDS

FINANCIAL OBLIGATIONS

FUNERAL RECORDS

INCOME SOURCES

INCOME TAX RETURNS FOR
   PRIOR YEARS

IMPORTANT CORRESPONDENCE

INSURANCE

INVESTMENTS

KEYS

LIST OF YOUR ASSETS

LEGAL RECORDS

MEDICAL INFORMATION

MARRIAGE CERTIFICATES

NATURALIZATION PAPERS

MILITARY RECORDS

NOTES RECEIVABLE

PASSPORTS

PROFESSIONAL ADVISORS
   (NAMES AND NUMBERS)

PROMISSORY NOTES

REAL ESTATE IMPROVEMENTS

REAL ESTATE RECORDS

SAFE DEPOSIT BOX
   RECORDS & KEYS

SAVINGS RECORDS
   (PASSBOOKS, ETC.)

SOCIAL SECURITY, CIVIL
   SERVICE, RAILROAD RETIRE-
   MENT OR OTHER GOVERN-
   MENT BENEFIT
   NUMBER & RECORDS

STOCKS

TAX RECORDS   VETERAN'S DISCHARGE PAPER
TITLE TO CEMETERY   OR CERTIFICATE
   PROPERTY

The complexities of the legal system as it relates to death make the average woman feel overwhelmed, like she's just enrolled in law school and is now the dunce of the class. The paperwork seems endless, the terminology is Greek, and there are a multitude of other worries pressuring you.

Remember, as we explain this process, not to berate yourself if it seems terribly complex or overwhelming. Especially if you are in the throes of grief, this probate business will seem impossible. It is expensive, time consuming and open to public scrutiny.

Who's Who or You Can't Know the Players Without a Program

If your husband died with a will, it is said that he died *testate*. If he died without a will, he died *intestate*. The person who makes a will is called the *testator*. The person named in the will to carry out the wishes of the testator is the *executor* (male) or *executrix* (female). Just because a widow is named in the will to be the executrix does not necessarily mean she has to do the job. You may not want to do the job or may feel too overwhelmed. You may also begin, but then find yourself no longer able to complete the task. In any of these cases, the court will appoint an *administrator* or *administratrix* for the estate. This could be another family member, friend, bank or an employee of the Public Administrator's office. Although the function is the same as the executrix, if the task falls to someone other than the person named in the will, that person is called the administratrix or administrator.

We will now discuss the various tasks involved in estate administration.

STEP 1: Where There's a Will, There's a Way
(But Without a Will, There's a Way, Too!)

The very first thing a widow must do is locate her husband's will. The family safe deposit box is the best place to start. Banks will not release the contents of a safe deposit box without a formal inventory by the appropriate public officials; however wills are an exception to this rule.

If you can't find your husband's will among the contents of a safe deposit box, try his office or home safe, fireproof metal box, etc. You will need to find the *original* will, one that is signed, dated and witnessed. A copy won't do. Statutory procedures for probating a lost or destroyed will vary from state to state. In some states, further search may not be necessary if probate is not required. If you're running into difficulties, seek legal advice immediately.

When you find the original will, naturally you will examine it immediately for funeral, burial and other special instructions. This is also the time to set up an appointment with your chosen probate attorney. She will help you interpret the other provisions of the will and to proceed with administration of the estate.

The will must be filed in probate court in the county and state where your husband was a resident at the time of his death. Generally, the will must be filed within ten days of the date of death. The clerk of the court normally acts as the court's custodian of wills, but a simple phone call to the court will determine the proper court official.

When you file the original will, you'll be given a receipt of deposit from the court. Keep this with a copy of the will in your file box.

If you have found no will and are certain there isn't one, you are automatically provided with the "will" the state has written for such cases. Laws of intestate succession vary from state to state. Your attorney will advise you of the rules of inheritance which apply in your state when there is no will. As we have said before in this chapter, you may not be happy with this turn of events but there is not a thing you can do about it now.

STEP 2: The "Data Bank" Roundup

Estate administration, whether or not there is a probate proceeding, will involve supplying lots of different people with lots of different information. We have referred earlier in this chapter to your Data Bank. Our list covered almost everything that is normally required, but in some cases it will not be comprehensive. Problems such as contested creditors' claims, will contests brought by dissatisfied heirs, or complex portfolios would normally require discovery of additional facts or documents.

STEP 3: Here Comes the Judge!

Determining whether or not a court proceeding is required is a critical step in the estate administration process. Each of the fifty states is a little different so we can't really give you a rule of thumb.

After you have completed STEPS 1 and 2, you should consult your probate attorney. Bring your Data Bank with you to the initial conference. From this information, she will be able to advise you if a court proceeding is necessary in your particular case.

If you think of the word probate as similar to the word "probe," it may help you identify what the process is all about. The purpose of probate is to probe or prove who should get what. Estate administration involves more than just the transfer of title. There is also the payment of valid creditors' claims, the collection of debts, the settling of any legal controversies, the payment of tax liabilities, and, finally, the transfer of property to those persons or entities entitled to receive it. Probate court merely supervises these functions under a complex statutory scheme. If a probate proceeding is not established, these matters should be taken care of without the supervision of the court.

If it is determined that a court proceeding is necessary, your own understanding of the probate process will help expedite matters. Your attorney won't have to spend so much time keeping you informed and you'll be better able to understand some of the intricacies and, often, delays of the proceeding.

If your attorney advises that a court proceeding is not necessary, you may choose to retain her or another professional person to prepare estate tax returns and handle related matters.

Let's suppose now that you have concluded an initial conference with your attorney. She tells you probate will be necessary. This is what you can expect to happen. Bear in mind, however, that many states have decedent administrative procedures regarding community property or property acquired by spouses during marriage which will differ from our example of a typical probate proceeding.

Just the Facts Ma'am

You may be wondering how it is that the probate court learns that your husband has died and probate should begin. Actually, you or your attorney inform the court that you need to start this legal process. You or your attorney will do this by filing a request known as a *petition*.

If you are named in the will as executrix, this petition will reflect your acceptance of the position. If your husband didn't leave a will, you may be asking to be appointed administratrix of the estate.

The petition will state facts which are necessary to establish the court's jurisdiction over the decedent's estate. These facts vary from state to state but generally the petition must show that the deceased was a resident of the state and county where the petition is filed. The petition must name all known heirs and beneficiaries of the deceased, including their residence addresses. It must set forth a summary of the assets of the estate and of course must prove a death has occurred.

In addition to these legal matters, the petition will include other facts relevant to the court proceeding and will normally conclude with a request that the petitioning party be appointed as estate representative (executrix or administratrix).

You may find the details required in the petition burdensome, yet each fact required has a statutory purpose; that is, it relates to some state or federal legal procedure. Due process and statutory law require that all persons and entities having a stated or potential beneficiary interest in the decedent's estate have notice of the probate proceeding. That means a notice must be mailed to the residence of each heir or beneficiary listed on the petition. The court requires proof that this has been done. Most states also require that notice be published in a local newspaper and some require posting of notice at the courthouse.

You may feel uneasy as each step seems to make your husband's death more and more public. Yet, through these initial probate procedures, interested parties are given the opportunity to express their interest and concerns to the court. Heirs and beneficiaries will naturally want to know what they will be getting under the terms of the will. They may also have some objections. Some of the grounds for objecting to a probate proceeding are:

1. Challenging the validity of the will and thus initiating a will contest;

2. Contesting the appointment of the nominated estate representative and seeking appointment of another party;

3. Refuting facts set forth in the petition as untrue or incomplete;

4. Challenging the jurisdiction of the court.

If any of the above objections is filed, a judicial proceeding, generally in the form of an evidenciary hearing, a trial by jury or by the court, or a hearing to argue legal issues, will be necessary. Naturally such proceedings result in delays to the probate procedure.

James and Other Bonds

Estate assets are summarized in the petition for two reasons.

First, you have to establish that the property is in the state of the court's jurisdiction before an estate representative will be appointed. Secondly, the executor or administrator must be bonded for an amount equal to the value of all personal property plus annual income, unless this requirement has been specifically waived in the will. Courts often will allow a reduced bond if the estate representative is the sole or principal beneficiary. However, even a reduced bond must be in an amount sufficient to protect potential creditors and taxing authorities.

The court determines the amount of the bond. The bond itself is usually arranged by the estate attorney. The premium in the bond, which in most states is regulated by law, is an expense of the estate.

After notice requirements have been met, and assuming there are no objections to the proceedings, the court will review the petition. If the court finds any procedural defects, there will be a delay in the probate process while your attorney makes the necessary corrections. When the court has reviewed and approved the petition, there will be a short and simple hearing appointing you, the nominee in the petition, as estate representative and setting the bond if one is required.

As estate representative you are now empowered to administer your husband's estate. This can be a big responsibility. Like a trustee or other legal agent, you are a fiduciary to the parties who will benefit from the estate. A breach of this fiduciary duty can result in financial liability to anyone damaged as a result of the breach. This simply means you must manage the property of your husband's estate with the same diligence and care that you would if it were your own. If there is any loss in assets due to your negligence, recklessness or intentional wrongdoing, you are liable to the other beneficiaries of the estate for the money you lost them.

Secondly, you must exercise the highest good faith and loyalty in carrying out your duties. You are legally bound to think first of the estate and its beneficiaries and not your own interests, whether or not you are the principal beneficiary. If you have any questions whatsoever about "conflict of interest," consult your attorney immediately for a legal opinion.

In fact, as soon as you are appointed estate representative, you should meet with your attorney. At this time you can calendar and divide up responsibility for every activity which will occur in the course of probate administration. Working closely with your attorney is the best way to stay out of trouble in your new fiduciary role.

You Thought You'd Outgrown Allowances

You are entitled by law to living expenses while your husband's estate is being administered. This is called the "family allowance." Rules governing the distribution of the family allowance vary from state to state. Generally, the widow, minor children and adult children who are physically or mentally incapacitated and dependent on the decedent for support are entitled to reasonable income maintenance out of the estate.

The amount you will get for living expenses is determined by the court. It depends on your customary standard of living, other current sources of income, and your specific needs. In some cases, a widow's right to family allowance may be affected by the terms of her husband's will. Or she may elect to inherit under the will rather than take any allowance for living expenses while the will is being probated.

Pay As You Go

One of the primary purposes of probate is to protect the rights of parties, other than natural heirs and beneficiaries, who have legitimate claims against your husband's estate. These are usually creditors, people your husband owed some money to at the time he died. It also includes taxing authorities. Taxes will be discussed a little later on in this chapter.

One of your first tasks as estate representative is to notify creditors that your husband has died and that they may file claims to be paid back from his estate. There are legal requirements for how to do this. Usually notice must be published in a local newspaper and posted at the courthouse. Sometimes you have to send notices by first class mail to creditors that you know of. Your attorney will help you with specific notice requirements.

Creditors will have a certain period of time in which to file written claims with the court. This varies from state to state, but usually it is four months from the date of first publication of notice. Written creditors' claims must explain the amount of money your husband owes and the reason why. Then you, as estate representative, must decide whether the claim is valid. If you reject a claim, and the creditor decides he wants to, he can file a civil law suit to recover the debt. As an alternative to outright rejection of a claim, you can usually seek the court's instruction on what to do about a particular debt.

When you approve a claim, it must be submitted to the court for review and approval. If the court objects for some reason, the matter is resolved by court hearing, if necessary, before the claim is paid.

It's important to work closely with your attorney during this procedure. If you pay a creditor's claim not specifically approved by the court, you may be held personally liable for the amount of the claim.

Getting It Together

In your data bank you began identifying all the assets of your husband's estate. Now you must prepare a detailed descriptive list or inventory of all these assets and give it to your attorney. She will then prepare a formal inventory document for submission to a court designated appraiser. The appraiser is the one who gives a formal value to every asset in the estate. When the appraiser is finished, the inventory document will be filed by your attorney with the court. The time period allowed to complete this process varies from state to state.

The inventory and appraisement document has several functions. First of all, it serves as the basis for accountability. As estate representative, you are responsible to the court, and, indirectly, to claimants and distributees of the estate, for proper management of all the assets set forth in the inventory and appraisement.

Secondly, this document also serves as the basis for determining statutory estate representative and attorney's fees. We will talk more about these later.

And finally, the inventory and appraisement document is usually relied upon by taxing authorities to compute the estate tax liability.

Getting It Settled

In addition to resolving creditors' claims, other legal disputes may have to be settled before final termination of a probate proceeding. Virtually any kind of civil litigation matter in which your husband could have been involved during his life can arise during probate of his estate.

Examples of litigation matters which can affect probate are:

1. A wrongful death action against parties negligently responsible for the death of the decedent.

2. Partition actions to recover decedent's interest in property jointly held.

3. Collection actions to recover debts owed by decedent prior to death.

4. Defense matters in which decedent's estate is named as a party defendant.

As estate representative and fiduciary, it is your duty to defend the estate in actions brought against it and to prosecute actions to recover money or assets owed to it. Normally you and your attorney will seek the court's approval before initiating any civil law suit. The court will want to assure appropriate legal representation, if necessary. The court also has an interest in minimizing litigation in order to prevent prolonged and costly probate proceedings. Civil law suits will normally affect both the taxable and distributable estate, as well as creditors' rights in some instances. For this reason, law suits generally must be resolved before a probate proceeding can be terminated.

Getting It to Uncle Sam

The most complicated part of estate administration is taxation of the estate. The following description is very simplified. We want you to have a general idea of what's going on but caution you that this explanation makes it sound a lot easier than it really is. Do not try to handle this aspect of estate administration on your own. At no time in the probate process is it more important to have the expert guidance of an attorney.

Your husband's estate, as represented by a court-appointed representative (you), is a taxable entity. You might think of it as a taxable "citizen." In order to become registered with taxing authorities, you need to acquire an estate tax number through the Internal Revenue Service. A similar requirement for registration is found in many states. Once obtained, the estate will be identified by this number in the same way that an individual is recognized, computerized and categorized by her social security number.

As a taxable entity, your husband's estate is subject to the same taxes and tax reporting requirements as individuals. Thus, if estate assets generate sufficient annual income, federal and state income tax returns must be filed. Virtually any kind of federal, state or local tax may be levied against an estate. And, in addition to tax systems designed for living persons, the federal government, as well as most state governments, have enacted a so-called "death tax" which is unique to decedent estates.

A comprehensive explanation of estate taxation is beyond the scope of this book. However, the following comprises an inventory of more common financial facts and events which give rise to tax reporting requirements:

- If the annual income of the estate is $600.00 or greater, a federal fiduciary income tax return must be filed;

- If a federal income tax return is required, a state income tax return may also be required;

- If the estate includes a business enterprise as an asset, then the same informational and substantive returns will be required that were required previously;

- If the estate includes real property, real property taxes must be paid according to state law where the property is situated;

- If the estate sells property, a local sales or transfer tax may be owed;

- If a boat, aircraft, motor home or automobile belongs to the estate, an annual personal property or use tax may be levied by the state where such vehicles are registered;

- If the estate paid employee wages during the fiscal year, federal and state employer taxes will apply.

The IRS and most state taxing authorities provide informational booklets and free advice to taxpayers on request. You may discover these to be a valuable resource.

As mentioned earlier, the federal government and most state governments extend special consideration through the so-called "death tax." The event which triggers this tax is, in fact, the death of a person, and all property in which the deceased had an ownership or beneficial interest at date of death, as well as property given away prior to death without fair market value consideration, is probably subject to the tax.

The federal estate tax, rather than the comparable state inheritance tax, constitutes the greater tax liability for estates which are large enough to be subject to this tax. It is an extremely complex and difficult tax system and bearing in mind that you, the estate representative, will be accountable for potentially heavy penalties and interest charges for a late or incomplete filing and delinquent tax payments, you would be foolhardy indeed not to seek professional help if you think the filing of a federal estate tax return may be required.

Regarding the federal estate tax, the threshold and most important question for you to answer is whether or not the estate is large enough to require the filing of a federal estate tax return. Because only "large" estates are subject to the tax, you may be able to accurately and easily determine if a return is necessary. If, however, one is clearly required or if your valuation of estate assets raises a doubt that the estate may be large enough to require the return, then we strongly urge you to have the estate professionally appraised and the return professionally prepared.

To resolve the threshold question, you must determine if the gross estate, at death, is equal to or exceeds the following values during the year indicated in this chart:

YEAR	VALUE
1979	$147,000.00
1980	$161,000.00
1981 and after	$175,000.00

By way of explanation the ascending "cut off" value is a major product of the 1976 Tax Reform Act. While increasing the amount of property which passes free of the federal estate tax, the 1976 Reform Act also increased the tax rate for gifts during lifetime by creating one uniform tax rate for both gifts and death transfers. One primary purpose of these major changes, along with other sigificant changes of the 1976 Act, is to decrease the tax burden of medium-size estates.

What constitutes a decedent's gross estate? The main category of property included is property, real and personal, and tangible and intangible in which decedent had full or partial ownership when he died. The property is included only to the extent of actual ownership at time of death. Thus, in community property states only one-half of the community property is included in the gross estate of the first deceased spouse.

A second major category is property in which decedent

had a beneficial interest, even though title or possession is held by another, such as a trustee or pledgee. The principal example of such "beneficial property" is a trust wherein decedent, prior to his death, transferred title to certain property to a trustee for the beneficial use of decedent during his lifetime.

A third major category is the value of all gifts subject to a gift tax made during decedent's lifetime. The obvious reason for this inclusion is to allow the Treasury to discover items of property subject to the gift and federal estate tax. As estate representative, you do not have the prerogative to exclude a lifetime gift because, in your opinion, it is not subject to the tax. A brief factual statement may be included supporting your view of exclusion from tax liability but the final judgment belongs to the IRS. All gifts of $1,000.00 or greater made within three years of death and all gifts of $5,000.00 or greater during lifetime must be included.

A fourth category is the proceeds of insurance on a decedent's life. This includes proceeds payable to the estate representative or to other beneficiaries providing your husband possessed incidents of ownership in the policy at his death.

While similar in form to life insurance, an annuity is ordinarily not included in the gross estate because the benefits terminate on death. But an annuity for a term of years which hasn't expired at time of death or one for the life of another joint annuitant is includable.

In computing the gross estate, we suggest you prepare a detailed inventory of assets in which your husband's estate may conceivably have an ownership or beneficial interest; include any and all gifts made by your husband as stated above. Next the market value of the estate at date of death must be determined. If fair market value of any assets is unknown or entirely speculative you should obtain a professional appraisement. If there is reason to believe a federal estate return may be required, you should hire a probate attorney or other professional tax preparer. You will have accomplished as much as any prudent person can accomplish and any other course of action would risk big problems with the IRS and significant losses to the estate through penalties and interest charges for improper or late filing and delinquent payment of taxes.

Assuming you have determined a federal estate return is required and have therefore retained an attorney or other professional tax preparer, what can you anticipate before the estate tax is determined and settled?

First of all, substantial data collection regarding assets, deductions and informative facts may be necessary. This phase of the process will hopefully be minimized as a result of the records system you have previously compiled.

Secondly, the return itself must be prepared. A professional tax preparer is crucial not only to assure accurate reporting of assets but also accurate and complete deduction claims. Deductions include administration expenses, debts existing and unpaid at date of death, unpaid taxes which occurred prior to death, losses, charitable bequests, orphan's inheritance for minor children and the marital deduction.

If you have minor children, the orphan's deduction may be significant to the tax picture if your husband has provided for them through an outright bequest or trust. The charitable deduction will of course apply only if your husband provides for qualified charities in his will. Standard deductions, i.e., expenses, debts and taxes, may or may not be significant, and the treatment of these deductions may be important in that the deductions may be defined as income tax deductions for better overall tax treatment.

The "marital deduction" may be very important to you as a surviving spouse. As amended by the 1976 Tax Reform Act, your husband can transfer to you the greater of one half of his gross estate or $250,000.00 free of any federal estate tax. The amount of the marital deduction will be reduced through an adjustment of the gross estate, in community property estates where one-half of all property acquired during marriage is considered yours. The "marital deduction" may also be reduced by gifts made to you by your husband before his death. However, the marital deduction, as you can readily see, may be very important in reducing federal estate tax liability.

A third event in the process is the filing itself or rather the timeliness of the filing of the return. Federal estate tax returns must be filed nine months from the decedent's date of death. Although extensions can be obtained from the IRS for good cause, the failure to file by the prescribed date results in the assessment of heavy late penalties and interest charges which may be returned only after an involved appeals process.

We come to the bottom line question: what is the tax rate? Keeping in mind that the taxable estate is the gross estate less deductions, including the "marital deduction," here is the Unified Estate and Gift Tax Rate Table:

Over	But Less Than	Tentative Tax =	+ %	Of Over
$ 0	$ 10,000	$ 0	18	$ 0
10,000	20,000	1,800	20	10,000
20,000	40,000	3,800	22	20,000
40,000	60,000	8,200	24	40,000
60,000	80,000	13,000	26	60,000
80,000	100,000	18,200	28	80,000
100,000	150,000	23,800	30	100,000
150,000	250,000	38,800	32	150,000
250,000	500,000	70,800	34	250,000
500,000	750,000	155,800	37	500,000
750,000	1,000,000	248,300	39	750,000
1,000,000	1,250,000	345,800	41	1,000,000
1,250,000	1,500,000	448,300	43	1,250,000
1,500,000	2,000,000	555,800	45	1,500,000
2,000,000	2,500,000	780,800	49	2,000,000
2,500,000	3,000,000	1,025,800	53	2,500,000
3,000,000	3,500,000	1,290,800	57	3,000,000
3,500,000	4,000,000	1,575,800	61	3,500,000
4,000,000	4,500,000	1,800,800	65	4,000,000
4,500,000	5,000,000	2,205,800	69	4,500,000
5,000,000	—	2,550,800	70	5,000,000

As you can see, the lowest percentage rate is eighteen percent and the highest is seventy percent! You are probably thinking, "thank goodness for the marital deduction," as well you should. There is, however, an additional factor in the computation of the federal estate tax which may be equal with the marital deduction in importance.

We refer to the so-called "unified credit" which has replaced the pre-1977 $60,000 exemption. Under the unifed credit system, every decedent's estate is credited with the payment of a certain amount of taxes which is applied as a credit against taxes due under the unified rate table. The amount of the unified credit is increasing each year but will stabilize in 1981. The following table indicates the unified credit and also the amount of property which passes tax free when the credit is subtracted from the taxable estate:

Year	Credit	Tax Free
1979	$38,000.00	$147,333.00
1980	$42,500.00	$161,563.00
1981 and after	$47,000.00	$175,625.00

The fourth and final step we identify as the processing of the federal estate return by the IRS. While the computation of tax is a part of the return, the IRS will in most cases carefully review the return including the computation of tax. Also, the incidence of IRS audits on estate returns is higher than on income tax returns probably because of the large taxes at stake. Disagreements with the IRS can of course be challenged through procedures similar to income tax returns.

Primarily because of the marital deduction and unified credit, federal estate tax liability of your husband's estate should be nothing to minimal if the gross estate is $450,000.00 or less. This is true because, assuming your husband dies in 1979 with a $450,000.00 gross estate and designates you as his sole beneficiary, the maximum marital deduction of $250,000.00 would reduce the taxable estate to $200,000.00. Referring to the Unified Estate and Gift Tax

Table, the tax on $200,000.00 is $38,000.00 plus 32% of $50,000.00 for a total tax of $54,000.00. However, the unified credit for 1979 of $38,000.00 reduces the tax liability ($54,000.00-$38,000.00) to $16,000.00. Other deductions, such as administrative costs, debts, etc., would reduce the taxable estate to a lower figure, and if these estate facts occurred in 1981, the unified credit of $47,000.00 would apply.

In addition to the federal decedent estate tax, most states have enacted a decedent estate tax system of their own. A few of them are based on the federal system. They tax the right to *transfer* property. But most states have what is called an *inheritance* tax. This is a tax on the right to *inherit* property.

The state inheritance tax rate is determined in two steps.

1. Identify the total value of all property being distributed to each beneficiary.

2. Identify the relationship of the beneficiary to the decedent.

A separate tax rate applies for each level of relationship. In general, the closer the relationship, the higher the basic exemption and the lower the tax rate. Wives and children pay less state inheritance tax than cousins or aunts (assuming the same amount of money is inherited).

Whether or not the decedent estate tax in your state is based on the federal or "inheritance" tax system, the rate will be quite a bit less than the federal estate tax rate. For example, the *lowest* tax rate under the federal system is greater than eighteen percent (after deducting the unified credits). The *highest* tax rate in most states is less than twenty percent. And the tax rate to a surviving spouse normally begins at three percent and goes to fifteen percent.

A final word of caution. "A little bit of learning is a dangerous thing." There are many factors we have not covered in this section which may substantially alter the tax consequences we have discussed. If your husband's estate is large enough to require the filing of a federal estate tax return, you need the assistance of an attorney to be sure this is done properly.

Giving and Getting

After creditors' claims have been settled and paid, any legal disputes have been resolved, taxes determined and paid, and all these matters have been accomplished to the satisfaction of the court, you are ready for final distribution of the estate.

Unless all your husband's beneficiaries waive this right, you, as estate representative, must make a final accounting to the court. This accounting accompanies your petition of distribution and reports in detail all transactions which have occurred during the course of estate administration. If the estate has gone up or down in value, you must explain why.

The accounting generally includes a request for fees for both the estate representative (you) and your attorney. Each state has its own laws governing the maximum amount that can be requested. Fee scales vary dramatically. In all states, however, the larger the estate, the smaller the *percentage* of fee allowed.

California is probably close to the average in fees allowed. Bear in mind that your state may be much higher or much lower than this chart shows.

Schedule for Computation of
Statutory Commissions for the Representative and
Statutory Fees for the Attorney
Under California Probate Code Section 901

Estate of $1,000 or less, 7 per cent of total Estate.

Estate of $1,000 to $10,000, 4 per cent of total, plus $30.

Estate of $10,000 to $50,000, 3 percent of total, plus $130.

Estate of $50,000 to $150,000, 2 percent of total, plus $630.

Estate of $150,000 to $500,000 1½ per cent of total, plus $1,380.

Estate of $500,000 and over, 1 percent of total, plus $3,880.

Alone

Under the California system, if your husband's estate were $1,000,000, the estate representative and the attorney would each be entitled to $13,880 [1% of $1,000,000 = $10,000 + $3,880, or $13,880].

In addition to statutory fees, you or your attorney can petition for additional fees for "extraordinary services." Most courts have guidelines to determine what is considered "ordinary" and what is considered "extraordinary." This will differ from state to state.

After the petition for distribution has been approved by the court, you will be discharged from your duties as estate representative. When this happens, the lengthy and complicated probate process will be complete.

Whether you administered your husband's estate or someone else did, whether it was supervised by the court or not, when it's all over, you'll have mixed emotions. It's another ending. And it's another beginning. We hope it will be a landmark on your road to recovery.

After seven years in operation, the San Diego, California, Widowed to Widowed Program has created an impressive document called a "Recovery Guarantee." While it is nothing that could be held legally binding in a court of law, it is meant to sound like a contract to insure the participant's commitment to working toward adjustment. There are a few items you could only do if you lived close to San Diego or some other city with a similar program (they are few and far between!). Most of the items, however, can be applied by widows everywhere. As a matter of fact, a number of these suggestions are equally applicable to any person going through stress. Why don't you look it over and see if it looks helpful to you? You might even enter into a similar contract with someone who cares about your well being.

THE WIDOWED TO WIDOWED
ONE-YEAR RECOVERY GUARANTEE

The Widowed to Widowed Program hereby guarantees almost complete recovery from the normal problems of grief and widowhood within one year if the participant complies with the following stipulations.

FINANCIAL AND LEGAL WELL BEING

1. Keep careful records of all your transactions. Photo copy all forms before sending them off and note where and when you sent them. Keep all documents received as well as carbons of your replies.
2. Maintain a written log of all the people you talk to on the phone concerning business, legal and financial matters (the bank, social security, mortuary, your lawyer). Include in your log a summary of your questions and their answers.
3. Set up a bookkeeping system that you can live with. Include in this some budget calculations concerning your regular expenses.

MENTAL WELL BEING

4. At least once, carefully read the booklet "On Being Alone." (This booklet is available through the American Association of Retired Persons (AARP). Contact your local chapter for a copy or write Widowed Persons Service, 1909 K Street, Washington, D.C., 20049).
5. Read at least five books related to widowhood and grief so that you are knowledgeable about the normal course of this life event.

PHYSICAL WELL BEING

6. Establish or maintain habits conducive to good health. These should include regular well-balanced meals, drinking plenty of water, getting regular moderate exercise and following a satisfactory sleep pattern.

7. Learn and use at least one relaxation technique that works for you. This may be self hypnosis, biofeedback, transcendental meditation, yoga or something else acceptable to you.

8. Avoid excesses in any habits. Do not drink more coffee or alcohol, eat more sweets or suddenly go on a crash diet, smoke more cigarettes, or do anything else more than you did before your loss. This applies to extreme busyness or extreme inactivity as well.

PSYCHOLOGICAL WELL BEING

9. Keep either a written journal or tapes of your experiences and feelings during this year. Include recollections of dreams, random thoughts and letters you will never send.

10. Maintain or cultivate a close friendship with at least one person whom you are able to call at two o'clock in the morning because you need to talk and they will listen without criticism.

11. Work on an album, scrapbook or some other project which will help you crystalize and preserve the memories of your spouse for yourself and children, grandchildren and friends. While you savor these memories, realize that life is going on and you are closing the door on the past to open new doors.

12. Listen politely to friends, relatives, and neighbors giving advice. Note all the pressures that are being made on you but resolve to make no major decisions unless they are absolutely necessary.

13. Continue or find at least one pleasurable treat in your life which you can enjoy at least weekly. This could be a hobby, sport, club or organization, going out to lunch, or taking a special trip as long as it is something that you truly enjoy and that you will be able to treat yourself to regularly. This is a difficult time and you deserve to pamper yourself.

14. Treat unsolicited advice and pressures from others as water off a duck's back. You may listen politely and attentively but resolve not to make any major decision within this year unless absolutely necessary. Be especially wary of business ventures with friends or relatives.

15. Give yourself permission to cry. Do not give yourself negative messages such as "not here in front of these people. . ." or "I am only feeling sorry for myself." Let the tears flow. There is nothing more therapeutic than a "good cry."

16. If you become concerned about your state of mind, you think you are "going crazy," or you find yourself contemplating suicide, seek professional help immediately. Don't stop until you find a counselor you feel comfortable with. Keep working with your counselor, be he or she a psychiatrist, psychologist, social worker, pastor or whomever, until you have worked through your problems and set new goals. People who use professional help when they need it are smarter and saner than those who don't!

SOCIAL WELL BEING

17. Participate in at least seven activities of the Widowed to Widowed Program.

18. Read at least one book on assertiveness and preferably enroll in a course in assertiveness training. Be honest with your friends, neighbors, relatives, and fellow employees. If you are going through a particularly difficult time, let them know. If they are doing—or not doing—something and it is upsetting you (such as not talking about your spouse), let them know what you would prefer. If you really want to be left alone or included in something, let them know. You cannot expect people to be mindreaders. Even though your need may seem very obvious to you, give people the benefit of the doubt by spelling it out to them. Remember! Communication is not easy even in the best of times.

Alone

PHILOSOPHICAL WELL BEING

19. If you are a member of a church or religious group, spend some time learning more about their philosophy concerning the final stage of our life cycle, death. If you are not a member of such a group and do not find one you can comfortably fit into, spend time fitting the reality of death into your own philosophy of life.

THE UNDERSIGNED HAS READ AND PROMISES TO CONSCIENTIOUSLY COMPLY WITH THE ABOVE STIPULATIONS OF THIS GUARANTEE. IF ONE YEAR FROM THE DATE OF THE SIGNING OF THIS AGREEMENT, LIFE DOES NOT LOOK ONE HUNDRED PERCENT BRIGHTER, THE UNDERSIGNED IS ENTITLED TO A COMPLETE REFUND OF THE PURCHASE PRICE OF THIS CONTRACT.

Date _____   _____
                              Your Signature

Putting your financial house in order

The topic of this chapter is much more emotionally charged than sex, religion and politics combined. We are going to be talking about your money and how you handle it. If you have absolutely no emotional hangups about money, this chapter will cause neither palpitations of your heart nor butterflies in your stomach. Beads of perspiration will not form on your forehead nor will your mouth get dry. If, on the other hand, money is a touchy subject to you, this chapter is bound to hit a few nerves.

That secure feeling you once had is gone. The future is full of questions. How much am I going to get? Will I be able to keep the house? What about my kids? Can I afford the little (or big) luxuries? Right now the future probably seems very frightening. You may be one of the many women who have never had the opportunity to control their own finances. You may have absolutely no idea how things stand. What you are most afraid of is the *unknown*.

It is healthier to confront your worst fears rather than permit them to haunt you as ghosts. Are you picturing yourself barefoot, in rags and begging for a crust of bread? Are you fearing you'll end up on welfare? Is there a soup line or "poor house" in your worst fantasy? These dark, dreaded fears are called "catastrophic expectations."

If you examine what you consider the "bottom of the barrel," your fears will diminish. If you don't admit your worst fears, you may spend the rest of your life fighting a nonexistent wolf at your door.

To diminish your fears, it's important for you to find out as soon as possible exactly how things stand. The legal proceedings of probate and divorce will force you to do this. Yet, it's important to recognize that this is also something you're doing for yourself. Like it or not, this next period in your life is going to be lived as a single woman. One of the best ways to take a positive step forward into this new life is to get your finances firmly under control.

We have all been pretty much accustomed to looking to a man for security. Perhaps you went straight from your father's household to your husband's. When you find yourself suddenly single, it may be tempting to continue this mental habit and to look at the months ahead as merely a "waiting period." You picture it as a "temporary" time between one man's security and the next. You may say to yourself plaintively, "I'll do the best I can," and then reassure yourself by adding, "If I really blow it, Mr. Right will come along just in time and bail me out." You may even plan to lean once again on dad or perhaps on sons and brothers "until I get back on my feet." You may really mean "indefinitely."

We cannot stress too strongly the pitfalls of this kind of thinking. Realistically, Mr. Right may never come along, or he may turn out to be Mr. Wrong if he does. That "waiting period" may very well turn into the "rest of your life." Before you shake your head and say, "That'll never happen to me," remember this. *When the turmoil of your present situation is behind, you will not be the same person you are now.* You will be stronger, wiser and more mature. You may even begin to relish the idea of independence and self-reliance. In most cases, this is *exactly what happens.* We want to emphasize that the cornerstone to true independence and self-reliance is financial security.

A good feeling about yourself and your future isn't something that just happens. It takes planning and discipline. You must assume the mental attitude that you will accept responsibility for your own future. If you haven't yet "grown up" about money matters, start *right now* to develop this attitude in yourself. Sweep aside all your old concepts about yourself and money. Read this chapter confidently and seriously, as if your whole future depended on it. It does.

We will start where you are now, by looking at the combined assets, liabilities, income and expenses of you *and* your husband. Then we'll talk about some of the changes to expect during and after a probate or divorce proceeding. Finally, we'll talk about what to do when it's all over and you're in charge!

First, a word to those who are contemplating divorce. If a great deal of property is involved, your attorney will spend a substantial amount of time analyzing your financial situation to determine what properties are owned by you and your husband together. Your attorney will also work hard to determine what value should be placed upon them. From this analysis, you and your attorney will determine what is reasonable in the way of a settlement, and what is necessary in the way of temporary and permanent alimony and child support. In order to operate efficiently, you must have access to records. Even in the most hostile divorce, it is possible to get information and records from your husband by legal deposition and interrogatory procedures. These are costly and time consuming. If you are now in possession of records, particularly cancelled checks, income tax returns, accounting books for a business, savings account passbooks, or the like, by all means keep them in your possession. *Do not pack up and leave without them. Do not allow your husband to pack up and leave with them.* The importance of record possession cannot be stressed too strongly.

If your husband is the strong, silent type and you have had absolutely no idea what's going on, let alone where to look for records, start with a copy of last year's income tax return. You will need some help interpreting the information but much of what you need to know will be there.

There are basically two ways that your financial condition

(or that of a corporation, business or partnership) can be analyzed. Each procedure has a different purpose and will produce different yet valuable information. We will liken these two ways to the family photo album and home movies. Let's say you wanted to record the financial events in your life on film. You would want to take a snapshot each year to show how things look in general. That is the same as determining your net worth at a given time. You do this by subtracting all of your liabilities from all of your assets. You find that having a family portrait once a year is insufficient so you take movies to catch the action that goes on. You want to have this motion picture to see how things are changing between one snapshot and the next. The movies are like looking at monthly income and expenses.

Your Net Worth

Most businesses are required to prepare a *Statement of Net Worth* annually. Most individuals or married couples do this only when they are required to for a special purpose such as applying for a loan. If you are facing divorce or probate, you will have to determine your net worth in order to settle your legal affairs.

If your particular situation is very complicated, attorneys and accountants will be helping you. This chapter will give you a general idea of the procedure that is followed. Once you catch on, we hope this is something you will want to do annually. Why not resolve to do it each year on your birthday? That way you can't forget.

Assets are technically defined as "the entire property of all sorts of a person, association, corporation, or estate applicable or subject to the payment of his or its debts." In other words, your assets are the things you own.

Your assets can be grouped loosely into five different categories: (1) Cash (2) Notes Receivable (3) Securities, Investments and Other Business Participations (4) Tangible Personal Property (5) Real Estate.

Determining the value of some assets is difficult. If you go through a probate or divorce, many of them will be officially valued or "appraised" by an expert. For right now, we will talk about how you can reach reasonable estimates on your own.

1. *Cash.* Cash assets are whatever you have in your checking or savings account. If you haven't had your savings account interest posted recently, now is a good time to go to the bank and bring your records up to date.

2. *Notes Receivable.* Money that is owed to you by another person is usually evidenced by a "promissory note." A promissory note in its simplest sense is merely a promise to pay. This note is called a "Note Receivable." An example would be money you are collecting on a second mortgage (or trust deed). Only the amount of money still owed is considered an asset (not the original amount of the note). If you don't already know, you should actually read the note and find out how often payments are made, whether they are interest-only, or principal and interest, and when the note will be paid in full.

3. *Securities, Investments and Other Business Participations. Securities* are discussed in more detail in the chapter on investments. It's relatively easy for you to determine the value of your own securities. If you've done a lot of investing, you probably have a stock broker who handles your account. If this is the case, the brokerage firm probably has the actual stock certificates or bonds for safekeeping. If not, these documents may be in a safe deposit box. To determine the value of the securities, call your broker, or any broker, and ask the current trading price of the stocks or bonds you hold. If the security isn't being actively traded, a broker should still be able to give you an approximate current trading price.

Investments and Other Business Participations will include any joint ventures or partnership in which you or your husband participate (i.e., investments in any form other than the simple lending of money). If your husband practices in a law firm, for instance, his participation in the firm will be in the form of a partnership interest. The best place to look for an approximate value will be in the financial statements of the venture. Look for the "book value" of the equity in the venture. (Beware, however, that book value doesn't mean what you can sell it for.) At the time of settlement in a divorce or probate proceeding, your attorney or accountant can help you determine the exact value by examining the appropriate business records.

4. *Tangible Personal Property* includes all your physical possessions, excluding real estate. Household possessions should be given minimal value. You know if you've ever had a garage sale, that sofas, lamps, beds and even televisions and stereo equipment have little resale value regardless of how much you paid for them. Under personal property you should also include automobiles (ask a car dealer or banker for the current "Blue Book" value), jewelry (you may need to have some things appraised by a jeweler), and collections (yours or your husband's), such as antique cars, stamps and artworks. You may estimate their value or have them appraised by an appropriate expert in the field.

5. *Real Estate* is any "real" property that you own. This means your own house (if you own it), and any other houses, buildings, or land you may have purchased. The value of real property is determined in a formal appraisal process by an expert who considers such things as original sale price, appreciation or depreciation, replacement costs, improvements, and recent comparable sales.

Here is an area where you may begin to flex financial muscles you never knew you had. Why not try your hand at appraising your house? You should be able to come up with a reasonable guess. Start by finding out what other houses in your neighborhood have sold for recently and adding or subtracting pluses or minuses in dollar amounts for attributes or faults unique to your place. You would give your house a plus dollarwise for such things as a swimming pool, nice landscaping, recent redecoration or remodeling, sprinkler system, corner lot, or good view. Minuses would be things that compare unfavorably with the houses you know that have sold in your neighborhood. Think of anything that would make your house less valuable to a prospective buyer such as run-down condition, only one bathroom, leaky roof or noisy street.

You can also talk to real estate agents in the area to find out what houses are selling for. This is especially wise if you haven't been comparing notes with your neighbors lately, if you've owned your house for a long time (ten to twenty years), or if no houses in your neighborhood have sold in the past six months. Real estate agents are usually more than happy to spend a few minutes chatting with you on the phone and can give you a rough idea of the market value of your home by description. Generally, they are anxious to serve you in the hopes you will list with them if you sell.

Once you have given this appraisal role a try, there may be no stopping you! If you have other real property besides your own home, you can use the same technique. For instance, if you own a vacant lot in another town, write to a real estate agent in that town, tell her you are considering selling the property and ask her what she thinks it's worth.

There is one final addition you may be making to your list of assets. You or your husband may carry "whole life insurance." Whole life insurance is an asset insofar as it has a "cash surrender value." Term life insurance is not an asset. For these purposes, it's sufficient to know how much life insurance is carried by you and your husband, in what form (term or whole life) and who are the beneficiaries. Life insurance is discussed in detail in our insurance chapter. This is also a good time to find out what other types of insurance you carry, such as medical, car and mortgage insurance.

If you have been doing what we have directed so far, you have now gathered all the information you can for your list of assets. There is one very tangible asset which you should now put at the very top of the list. *You* are your own primary priceless asset. Like the good will of a company, this is an asset to which you can't give a specific value, but it is an asset in which you have probably invested a great deal of time, money and interest. Don't undervalue yourself! Think of yourself as your own greatest asset because you are! Especially if you find yourself falling into the category of "displaced homemaker," it is important that you place a high value on yourself and your capabilities. You have years of earning power ahead of you and you will begin to cash in on this.

Now it's time to look at your "liabilities." These are the debts you have incurred to acquire your various possessions and to make investments which you hope will earn you more money. There are four general forms of liabilities. They are: (1) Current Bills (2) Installment Debts (3) Debts to Individuals (4) Mortgages (or Trust Deeds).

1. *Current Bills.* Anything you have to pay this month is a current bill. Consider things like gas, electricity, doctor, dentist, rent, telephone, etc.

2. *Installment Debts* include loans you took out when you bought your car, boat, refrigerator, etc. Money owed to department stores, credit unions, or Mastercharge, Bankamericard or Visa cards, student loans, etc., are considered installment debts. In most cases, you will receive a monthly statement showing how much you still owe. For your own information you should also find out (or remind yourself) how much longer you'll be paying on these debts and what interest rate you are paying.

3. *Debts to Individuals* include money you may have borrowed from the previous owner when you bought your home (a second mortgage or trust deed). You may also owe some money to friends or relatives. These debts may differ greatly. Some have no interest and informal repayment dates. (Maybe the fairy godmother in your family knew you were having a difficult time and said, "Here. Just pay me back when you can.") Some have interest payments due at regular intervals for a few years (three to five) and then the entire principal sum due at the end (balloon payment). Some may be for an extended period of time (ten years) with equal monthly payments that will gradually pay off both principal and interest by the end (this is called *amortization*).

Recordkeeping for loans between individuals is sometimes very casual. If you have any doubts about the amount you originally borrowed, the terms of repayment, the due date or whether or not the loan is being amortized, read the loan documents. (You probably have a copy of the note you signed somewhere. If not, the person you owe will have the original and can send you a copy.) If you need help interpreting the document, ask a knowledgeable person to help (accountant, lawyer, banker). If you are in doubt as to the present *balance* of the note, ask the person you borrowed from to prepare an up-to-date statement. If the note is being amortized and neither of you is sure how much of your past payments have gone to interest and how much to principal, a bank loan department, title insurance company, escrow officer, or even the public library, have amortization tables which are easy to use. All you need to know is the length of time on the loan, the interest rate and the original amount borrowed. Once your records are up to date, you'll do yourself a great favor to keep them that way on a monthly basis.

4. *Mortgages (or Trust Deeds)* represent by far the largest debt most of us will ever have in our lives. This is the money you borrowed to buy your home. As you may have noticed, especially during the first few years of the loan, each time you make a monthly payment, most of it goes to pay interest and only a small proportion decreases the principal amount of the note. The easiest way to find out how much principal you still owe is to check the latest loan statement you got from the bank or mortgage company. If you don't save them, or if your mortgage holder doesn't send them, call the loan officer and she will be glad to provide the information.

Unless you have some very unusual circumstance, that is it! You have your financial house organized into assets and liabilities. Subtract the liabilities from the total assets. The difference is your "net worth." We can be formal and call it a "Financial Statement" or a "Statement of Net Worth." Actually, it's a snapshot of how your financial profile looks right now. Sit back and take a look at it. If it's a good picture, the total assets will equal a lot more than the total liabilities.

If it's a bad picture, the net worth will be insignificant (less than $1,000), relatively low in comparison to income, or (rarely) a negative net worth.

If the picture is bad, you'll need to take a closer look at the details of the snapshot. You may even need a professional to take a look with you. Could you be saving more money to build up some assets? Are your assets worth the "carrying" costs (the money it costs to own them)?

In a crisis, you may need to sell something quickly to get back in financial shape. "Liquid" assets are cash or things which can be turned quickly into cash to meet an emergency. Something like a house takes time to sell. You need to list it with a broker, show it, find a buyer and put it through escrow. This may take anywhere from six weeks to six months. Real estate is not a liquid asset. Blue chip stocks, on the other hand, can be sold by one phone call to your stockbroker. You may have to sell at a time when you'd rather not, at a low market price, but you *can* find a buyer quickly if you have to. Marketable securities such as blue chip stocks are normally very liquid.

Assets are usually listed in order of liquidity. We have done so in this chapter by listing (1) Cash (2) Notes Receivable (3) Securities, Investments or Other Business Participations, and (4) Real Estate, in order of liquidity.

During a divorce proceeding your attorney will spend a great deal of time analyzing information about your assets and liabilities. You, your husband, and both attorneys must agree on the precise value of each asset. Sometimes this can be done informally, but if all else fails, the judge decides in court. If you live in a community property state, it is also necessary to establish whether the property in question is community or separate property. If there is a dispute, you and your husband must decide how any community property will be split. As with the valuation of assets, these matters can be settled beforehand or in court. Financial information must be constantly updated during the months or years the divorce is pending. Awards on property settlements differ, of course, from state to state and from judge to judge. For a rule of thumb, however, you will be very lucky if you get close to half of what is presently owned between you and your husband.

If you are experiencing widowhood rather than divorce, there is a different process. During probate your husband's assets will be formally valued and taxed according to statute. Liabilities will be paid where possible and necessary. Sometimes assets must be sold (liquidated) in order to pay these liabilities. Then, too, there is always the possibility you may not inherit all your husband's estate by the terms of his will or the provisions of your state if he died intestate (that is, without a will).

When the divorce or probate proceedings are finished, you will want to sit down again and draw up a list of your own assets and liabilities as a single woman. At that time the snapshot may look very different.

Income and Expenses

What about tomorrow, though? And the next day? And the bills at the end of the month? You need to know the answers to these pressing questions, too.

If you are getting a divorce, one of the first things your attorney will request is an estimate of your current living expenses in order to fix temporary alimony and support. It is crucial to estimate these figures as realistically as possible since final alimony and child support are often influenced by how much was paid in temporary support. Usually, you take the average of the past three years to establish normal living expenses. (Again, think how much easier this will be if *you* have the household records.)

Take a sheet of paper, label it "Monthly Income and Expenses" and draw a line down the middle. On one side put "Money In" (Income). On the other side put "Money Out" (Expenses). Depending on your circumstances you may wish to put only your *own* income and expenses. But if you're married, separated but not legally divorced, or only recently widowed, it may make more sense to list everything combined and then begin to think of how things can or should be divided up.

The income side will be fairly short. Put net monthly salary (actual take-home pay) and any other income you may receive such as interest dividends, payments from borrowers, etc. If you receive income on any basis other than monthly, prorate it. For example, if you receive $300 quarterly (four times a year) on stock dividends, multiply this by 4 to obtain how much comes in a year, divide the answer, or $1200, by 12 and enter $100. This is the portion that you actually receive each month.

The expense side may be a lot more detailed. Start first with your regular monthly expenses such as rent or mortgage payments, car loan payments, child care, utilities and phone. Then estimate such things as food (how much on meals at home? how much for lunch each day at work?), household items, transportation (to and from work, grocery store, doctor, etc., by bus? by car?), cosmetics, clothes for the family, and entertainment.

Be realistic. It's normal to underestimate entertainment expenses because we're psychologically reluctant to admit it when we spend money on ourselves "for fun." When you married, you discovered that two cannot live as cheaply as one. If you are reading this in contemplation of a divorce or death, remember one does not live as cheaply as "half a couple." *Especially* when you separate, expenses will increase.

Some expenses occur only a few times a year or annually, such as medical and dental expenses, car maintenance and repair, car registration, insurance premiums (car, life and medical), club memberships, state and federal income tax and property tax. Many of these expenses will vary from year to year, but they can be estimated from what you paid last year. If you're having trouble rounding up some of this information, a good place to start is by thumbing through last year's cancelled checks. How much did it really cost you to own and operate your car for a year? (This is usually a shock.) Divide all your annual expenses by twelve to get a monthly figure. Include this in your estimated monthly expenses. You should also include a "miscellaneous" monthly expense for such things as major home repairs (are your water heater and garbage disposal on their last legs? What about that worsening leak in the garage roof?)

When you've completed your list of income and expenses you will have a moving picture of your financial affairs. Unlike the snapshot Financial Statement, the Income and Expense Statement shows how the money flows from month to month (much like family members dart in and out of home movies!) If it's a good picture the monthly income will amply cover the monthly outgo with plenty left over for savings, vacations or investments. If it's not such a good picture (rated "X"), you will need to find some places to cut back before things get more out of hand.

You're On Your Own

The first year you are on your own as a divorcee or widow, your financial situation may fluctuate or alter dramatically from month to month. There will be a number of unusual bills for legal fees, funerals, trips, counseling, and child care. Your husband may or may not pay his alimony and child support on time. You may go to work for the first time. This will bring in more money but will also increase incidental expenses such as child care, working lunches and wardrobe improvements. You may move to a cheaper dwelling but incur moving expenses.

Your emotions in this very stressful period can cause you to wreak havoc on your budget. Beware of pressures that cause you to overspend. Boredom or depression may cause you to eat out a lot. Insecurity about your attractiveness may tempt you to spend money extravagantly on new clothes, accessories and cosmetics. Bitterness and hostility may send you on compulsive shopping sprees with your charge cards. Guilt may have you showering your kids with toys. Loneliness may send you on costly escape weekends to far away places. You may simply be accustomed to a higher lifestyle than is now realistic. It is normal to have some trouble breaking old habits. Maybe you can afford some of these extravagances. The chances are you can't afford all of them.

If you look at your income and expenses faithfully every month you will not be able to ignore any of the danger signals that tell you expenses are getting out of hand. Remember, one of the things we are working on in this chapter is your attitude towards money. As a mature adult, you have no excuse to indulge yourself in any of these stereotyped reactions. You're in charge now and responsible for your own financial security. Gradually, things will settle down. Your income and expenses as a single woman will become more patterned and predictable. You can begin some serious financial planning for the future.

Building Financial Security

Even during the best of times, we all seem to live pretty much from paycheck to paycheck. If you're living well, you probably do your discretionary spending at the end of each month when you can tell what's "left over." If you're just scraping by, you wind up eating peanut butter sandwiches the last four days of the month. You can usually find room on a charge card for unexpected car repairs or a necessary birthday or wedding present. You get by.

But what about those vague feelings of anxiety? Where does it all go? How come I can't ever seem to *save* money? How on earth am I going to afford a new car when this one breaks down? Even if you've never had to worry about money before, chances are you'll be asking yourself questions like this during the first year or two that you're alone.

The answer to all these questions is the same—a budget. We're going to take that movie camera we've been using and ZOOM IN for a close up look at exactly how your money comes and goes. Before you suddenly remember you had intended to defrost the refrigerator today, or you really do have some errands you need to run, stop a minute. Remember! The anxiety you are feeling will only go away when you stand fast and confront your worst fears. Maybe you *are* spending your money foolishly. Maybe it's even so bad you're literally "throwing" it away. *Knowing* that won't hurt you. It will *help* you, because then you can do something about it if you decide to.

Stand fast and let's look at your monthly budget. Take a sheet of paper and rule it into eight columns. Label them:
1. Food
2. Rent or Mortgage
3. Phone & Utilities
4. Household Expenses
5. Transportation
6. Clothing & Personal Care
7. Entertainment
8. Miscellaneous

If you have children, make a ninth column for:
9. Child Care

Every time you write a check this month, enter it in the appropriate column. Under (1) Food, list food purchased at the grocery store and meals eaten out. Under (2) Rent or Mortgage, put your monthly payment to your landlord or to the bank or mortgage company. Under (3) Phone & Utilities, put your monthly phone bill, gas, electric, water and other similar monthly charges. Under (4) Household Expenses, put any items having to do with running the house. These can be anything from major appliance repairs (your water heater finally broke!) to paying a gardener, buying chemicals for your swimming pool, replacing lightbulbs or buying cleanser and paper towels. Under (5) Transportation, put money spent for gas, car repairs, tune-ups, new tires, car insurance, parking, tolls, or bus or taxi fare. Under (6) Clothing & Personal Care put your own (and your children's) expenses for clothes, makeup, toothpaste, hair spray, etc. Under (7) Entertainment, put money spent on movies, theater, ballgames, club membership fees, trips to the zoo and so forth. Under (8) Miscellaneous put such things as children's music lessons, a vacation trip, medical and dental expenses (you may want to set up a separate column if these are frequent), dues for professional associations, courses you are taking, etc. If you have children, in your ninth column put (9) Child Care and include their nursery school charges or sitter care while you work or spend time away from them.

Enter each check you write this month in one of these columns. For example, suppose on the fifth of this month (we'll suppose it's January), you pay your rent with a check for $200. Enter $200 under (2) Rent or Mortgage, like this:

Date	Food	Rent or Mortgage	Phone & Utilities	Household Expenses	Trans portation	Clothing & Personal Care	Enter tainment	Miscel laneous
1-5		$200						

On the eighth of the month you write a check for the phone bill of $32.68. Enter $32.68 on the next line under (3) Phone & Utilities, like this:

Date	Food	Rent or Mortgage	Phone & Utilities	Household Expenses	Trans portation	Clothing & Personal Care	Enter tainment	Miscel laneous
1-5		$200						
1-8			$32.68					

On the tenth of the month you pay the water bill of $12 and send the exterminator a check for $15.88. Put the $12 under (3) Phone & Utilities and the $15.88 under (4) Household Expenses, like this:

Date	Food	Rent or Mortgage	Phone & Utilities	Household Expenses	Trans portation	Clothing & Personal Care	Enter tainment	Miscel laneous
1-5		$200						
1-8			$32.68					
1-10			$12.00	$15.88				

On the fifteenth of the month you cash a check for $50 and spend $5.75 on a luncheon date with a friend and $33.59 for lipstick, perfume, curlers and some other items for personal care at the drug store. Enter the $5.75 under (1) Food and $33.59 under (6) Clothing & Personal Care, like this:

Date	Food	Mortgage	Phone & Utilities	Household Expenses	Trans- portation	Clothing & Personal Care	Enter- tainment	Miscel- laneous
1-5		$200						
1-8			$32.68					
1-10			$12.00	$15.88				
1-15	$5.75					$33.59		

Remember the $50 check? You still have $10.66 left in cash. Remember to enter that when you actually spend it later on.

Money is much easier to keep track of if you pay by check and write little memory joggers in your checkbook about your purchase. When you spend cash, rather than writing checks, you'll have to train yourself for awhile to pay attention to where the money goes. Carry a little notebook with you in your purse, and jot down 75¢ for parking downtown, $2 to the office pool for Gloria's shower present, $1 for your son to buy a treat at the movie theater with his friends. Sit down faithfully each night before you go to bed, total your spending for the day and put it under the proper headings. Make this a regular habit.

If you do lose track of a couple of items or forget completely for a day or two, that does not give you permission to stop and "start over again next month." No excuses! Just pick up where you left off and strive to do better.

When the month ends, total each column across the bottom of the page. That will tell you how much money you spent that month in each of the categories.

Here is an example of a completed monthly spending record:

Date	Food	Rent or Mortgage	Phone & Utilities	Household Expenses	Transportation	Clothing & Personal Care	Entertainment	Miscellaneous	Total
1-5		$200							
1-8			$32.68						
1-10			$12.00	$15.88					
1-15	$ 5.75					$33.59			
1-16					$12.00				
1-18	$ 36.00						$15.50		
1-20	$ 24.00		$ 9.00						
1-25	$ 12.75			$14.36				$20.00	
1-29	$ 64.00				$12.00				
1-30			$ 6.00				$14.00		
Total	$142.50	$200	$59.68	$30.24	$24.00	$33.59	$29.50	$20.00	

We have made this budget very simple to use as an example. If this were your own, you would find that you had spent a total of $142.50 for (1) Food, $200 for (2) Rent or Mortgage, $59.68 for (3) Phone & Utilities, $30.24 for (4) Household Expenses, $24 for (5) Transportation, $33.59 for (6) Clothing & Personal Care, $29.50 for (7) Entertainment and $20 for (8) Miscellaneous. Now, add those all together and you'll find that you spent $539.51 for the month. If your "net income" or take-home pay were $600 you would have $60.49 left over to spend or save. That's pretty good.

Suppose, however, that you had also charged $58 for a new pair of shoes and had cocktails with a friend one evening which you charged, for $5.50. Your total for (6) Clothing & Personal Care would increase from $33.59 to $91.59 and your total for (7) Entertainment would be $25.50 instead of $20. When you add that extra $58 and $5.50, you find you have "spent" $603.01 for the month. That's $3.01 more than you take home! You can see that you may be headed for trouble!

Take a look at your own budget at the end of the first month. Do you see yourself heading for trouble? Are there any changes you'd like to make? Even if you have a little left over at the end, are you really adequately protected for an emergency? An unexpected trip home to be with an ailing parent? Emergency medical treatment? Or losing your job? What about your future plans? A vacation? Further education? You're not allowed to count on Prince Charming galloping in on a white charger. Remember! You're going to be responsible for your own financial future.

We need to add a ninth column to that budget next month and we will label it (9) Savings. We will plan to move money from one of the other columns and put it into this very important category, Savings.

Let's look at the sample budget again. Suppose you decided you really could eat out less often and shop more wisely at the grocery store. Your goal next month is to spend $125 on (1) Food instead of $142.50. Your (2) Rent or Mortgage will stay the same, $200. Your utilities are about average but you could eliminate a lot of those long distance phone calls, so you'll plan to spend $45 instead of $59.68 for (3) Phone & Utilities. You'll leave your (4) Household Expenses at about $30 and your (5) Transportation at $24. You'll try to keep your (6) Clothing & Personal Care to around $35 and your (7) Entertainment at $30. You decide that $20 is reasonable for (8) Miscellaneous. Add these all up and you get $509. With take-home pay of $600, that will leave a possibility of $91 for (9) Savings. If your own "savings muscles" have atrophied, you'll have to start flexing them slowly and build up. Even $10 or $25 a month is okay to start. The important thing is that you *start*.

Now, when you set up your budget for the next month, you have some realistic goals for what you wish to spend. Write these at the top of each column, like this:

Date	Food	Rent or Mortgage	Phone & Utilities	Household Expenses	Transportation	Clothing & Personal Care	Entertainment	Miscellaneous	Savings
	$125.	$200.	$45.	$30.	$24.	$35.	$30.	$20.	$91.

Now, when you write checks or spend cash, you can do some subtotaling along the way and make sure you stay within your goal.

Suppose on the fifth you spend $16 for groceries. On the eighth you have lunch out for $4.15 (total so far, $20.15). On the twelfth you spend $31 for groceries (total, $51.15). On the fifteenth you have dinner out for $8.75 (total $59.90). On the eighteenth you spend another $40.10 for groceries (total, $100.00). On the twenty-second your friend asks you to have brunch with her at her favorite restaurant downtown. You look at your budget.

Date	Food	Rent or Mortgage	Phone & Utilities	Household Expenses	Trans- portation	Clothing & Personal Care	Enter- tainment	Miscel- laneous	Savings
1-5	$16.00								
1-8	$ 4.15								
1-12	$31.00								
1-15	$ 8.75								
1-18	$40.10								

You've already spent $100 on food. Your goal is $125. You have nine days to go before payday. You know from last month's budget that you've been spending around $30 a week on groceries. You'll have to make one more trip to the grocery store before payday so you'd better pass on the brunch invitation and make sure you spend only $25 on your next trip to the grocery store.

Follow the same procedure for each category during the month. If you wind up spending more than the budget goal in a category before the month is over, that does not give you permission to quit your budget. Instead, notice whether your budget amount was realistic. Perhaps you really need to spend more money on food (or household expenses or transportation) than you had hoped. If so, you can raise the budget amount for the next month. If not, you should strive to discipline yourself and do better next month. A few failures are not an excuse to quit. Give yourself the time you need to learn new spending habits.

Many banks have automatic savings programs that can be very helpful. Money is transferred automatically from your checking account to your savings account at regular intervals. This works very well for some women who believe "You can't spend what you don't see!" Your savings account is your personal security for the future. You should think of it proudly as your key to independence! It is the initial step necessary to build toward long-range investments.

In addition to regular savings, sound financial planning demands that you predict expenses and *be prepared to meet them without emergency borrowing.* As you refine your budget techniques, you will want to set up a contingency fund, much like a savings account, to cover large expenses which occur only once or twice a year. Suppose your car insurance last year was $300. You guess that it will increase to $360 this year. You will want to set aside one/twelfth of that amount each month, $30 a month in order to pay the $360 bill when it arrives. (If you put the $30 into your savings account each month, you will earn interest on it while you are waiting.) Other expenses like this are state and federal income taxes, property taxes and homeowner's insurance.

If you anticipate receiving alimony, you should be aware that this is periodic income from which no income taxes are withheld. You will be required by the Internal Revenue Service to file quarterly payments of income tax on your alimony in January, April, June and September of each year on Form 1040ES. Your state may have a similar requirement. Consult an accountant immediately, advise yourself of the requirements and the amount she estimates you will need to pay each quarter, if any, and begin to set this money aside from each of your monthly payments.

Budgeting is a very personal matter. No two women will spend or save their money in the same way. Nor should they. The important thing is that you spend reasonably, cut back where possible or necessary and that you have some kind of planned program for building up your savings to meet emergencies and for those special things you want in your life someday.

By special things we do *not* mean extravagant "man-hunting" vacations or the "right" address and a status symbol wardrobe to attract the right man. Remember, you are planning for the rest of your life. Take some time to develop realistic, long-range goals to strive for. Perhaps you are tired of paying rent and want to own a home of your own in seven years. Maybe you want to finish your college education. Perhaps you want to start a new career and will need some special training. Or maybe your dream is to go into business for yourself. Goals like these, if they are realistic for you, will substantially improve the quality of your life even as you work towards them.

Now that you're single and in charge of your own finances, take a look at that revised Statement of Net Worth. If your assets consist simply of a car and perhaps some furniture, and your budget is limited, you must not be discouraged. You can still expect to meet realistic long-range goals by careful planning and saving. Your area of concentration will be where to cut back in an already tight budget so that you can add to your assets. Study your spending habits again. Are you wasting money on frozen foods or impulse purchases in the supermarket? (Surely you aren't grocery shopping when hungry!) Do you buy clothes you don't really need? Could you save money by going to garage sales or secondhand stores? Would you really be better off taking the bus for awhile rather than paying for gas, insurance and car repairs? How about your house or apartment? Can you really afford the rent? Should you move? Would you consider taking in a roommate for awhile? Any of these changes can and should be considered. You'll be surprised how easy disciplining yourself becomes with practice and when you can keep your attention clearly focused on a realistic long-range goal. The important thing is that you begin *now* to set aside money to make your dreams come true.

If you're one of the lucky ones with lots of assets, perhaps a home, car, some securities and shares in a business, other investments, and ample income, you will want to concentrate on protecting and increasing your assets. Begin with a sensible budget. (That means living well within your means.) Then spend some time learning about how to handle your money if you aren't already feeling confident in that area. A good place to begin is our chapter on investments!

Dollars and sense

Financial security is the cornerstone of your independence as a single woman. The foundation of your financial security will be planned spending and planned savings. We hope you will also want to build wisely on this foundation. You have the rest of your life ahead of you. Investing is a positive vote for your future. After all, if you thought there was no tomorrow, you'd spend it all today, right?

There's a clever little saying floating around these days: "You work for your money. Why shouldn't your money work for you?" This idea is as American as motherhood and apple pie. In this chapter we'll be talking about putting your available money to work for you.

Did you notice we said "available" money? The single most important thing to remember about investing is this. "If you can't afford to lose it, don't invest it." Money you invest is money you don't need for day-to-day living expenses, insurance, or your savings for emergencies.

A woman alone with money to invest soon discovers a world full of opportunities. Your next door neighbor feels he's an expert in tax shelters. Your friend's sister just got her real estate license. Your banker has been asking you to come talk to him for several weeks. Everybody has advice to give.

The world of investments can be confusing. It is also challenging, exciting, and a little bit scary. What *are* you going to do with that "nest egg" of yours?

109

Alone

A good place to begin is by asking yourself, "What are my goals?" "Getting married again", is not an acceptable answer! Remember your knight in shining armor may never appear. Then again, even if he does come galloping along, he may have no more investment sense than his mighty steed!

Women have many different investment goals. You may be thinking of your children's college education, retirement income, buying a home, redecorating a home, or quitting work to go see the world. Any goal is a good goal. The important thing is that you take some time and think about what you want your money to do for you.

Right now, take a piece of paper and write down briefly three specific goals that you have thought of. Now keep those in mind as you read the rest of this chapter.

Regardless of the specific reasons why you invest, basically you'll be looking for one of three things:

1. Growth,
2. Security, or,
3. A balance between the two.

Women who want investment growth will be willing to take some chances. Making a big return on your money (more than 15%) means taking risks. You can make a killing; but you can also be wiped out.

Women who invest for security will want very safe investments. They want simply to conserve their assets by keeping pace with inflation. They are not willing to take risks.

Many women opt for a balanced portfolio. Some of their investments are conservative; some are risky. They hope to come out ahead by playing on both sides of the fence. This is what is known as "hedging."

As we begin to talk about the world of investments and the opportunities available, some of them will be riskier than others. Notice where you belong. Some investments are for you, some are not. This is a decision we leave to you and your investment advisors.

Far from being something mysterious, investing is actually something you've been doing all your life. Did you have savings passbooks at your school? The nickels and dimes you deposited weekly were an investment. Perhaps you saved up part of your allowance or babysitting money for ballet shoes for your spring recital. This was investing in the future. If you own a home and have fine silver, china or jewelry, right now, they are investments. Anytime you put your money to work for you, it's an investment.

Maybe we should pause here and consider where hoarding and saving leave off, and investing begins. Every few years we read in the newspaper about some curious little old man who has just died. He's been living for the past twenty years in a filthy hovel surrounded by rampant weeds and mangy, stray cats. Upon his death, neighbors discover his mattress is literally stuffed with money. In the backyard they find thirty coffee cans, also stuffed with money, buried in the dirt. This is "hoarding." Often, hoarders can't bring themselves to spend money even when they really *need* to. Surely you will not be included among those eccentrics who die "penniless" with thousands of dollars tucked away? Money in mattresses and coffee cans just sits there, or mildews, or the cats nibble on it, or somebody steals it. Hoarded money can't work for you. Invested money does.

Now let's look at savings. Placing your money in an interest-bearing savings account can be considered an investment. The risk factor is minimal. The bank failure phenomenon of the 1930's is no longer a likelihood due to government-backed insurance. You've probably noticed signs or statements in your bank telling you your account is insured up to $40,000 by an agency of the federal government. Savings accounts are a very secure investment. But if the *risk* is small, the prospect of real *gain* is even smaller. If you have your money in a regular passbook account at 5½% interest and the inflation rate for the year is 10%, your money is losing ground! To add insult to injury, you probably had to pay some income tax on the interest you made. We are not suggesting that you withdraw all your funds from your savings institutions. There definitely is merit to having some of your money easily accessible. What we are suggesting is that if you are looking to a savings institution as your *only* investment plan, you need to find one in a country with almost no inflation and no income tax. The United States is not that country. If there is one somewhere, it probably doesn't honor motherhood and apple pie.

Our discussion about inflation may have dampened your enthusiasm. But you may have another investment which has been riding the upward spiral of inflation and even surpassing it. This is your house, the largest single purchase you will probably make in your life.

When you find yourself suddenly alone, you may begin to wonder if you should change your place of residence. If you own your own home and have lived there any length of time, every corner is filled with memories. There may be memories you want to cling to forever or memories you wish to discard as soon as possible. Emotional and economic considerations are very likely to conflict. Basically, hasty decisions at a time of emotional stress are later regretted. So our first suggestion is *go slowly*. If you are feeling emotional pain, you may think that a move will take you away from that pain. The pain is actually within you, so there is no place in the world you can go to escape it. Furthermore, the stress of moving and attempting to get oriented to a new neighborhood can be overwhelming.

Now that we have touched on the emotional aspects, we will shed some light on the investment aspects of home ownership. After that we will move on to other real estate investments.

First of all, unless you are catching a spaceship to another planet in the very near future, you have to live somewhere. This is the reason most people buy a house. When it comes to the question of whether to buy or rent, you must calculate the true, not the supposed, costs of ownership.

First, you should estimate your annual home-owning expenses. Besides mortgage payments, this sum includes taxes, insurance, assessments, and maintenance. You might include in your calculation the water bill and portion of heat and gas which you are sure you would not be consuming if you were renting. (If you are contemplating a rental situation, be clear on which utilities, if any, are paid by the landlord.) Now, stop and consider whether your house is "livable" as is or whether you feel remodeling or other improvements are necessary. Add the costs of these essential changes to your sum.

There is still more calculating which you must do. How much equity have you built up in your house? That is, how much money did you use to make a down payment and how much of your loan or loans have you paid off? What is the difference between the price you paid for the house and its fair market value today? Ask yourself one more important question: How much interest per year would you be making on this money if you had it in a savings account?

Now that you've been adding all these expenses up, we finally have a subtraction for you! What do you save on your income tax each year because of interest and property tax payments?

Have you arrived at an answer yet? We hope we didn't lose you in these mathematical gymnastics. You may want to have your accountant help you find the bottom line. If all goes according to plan, you should be able to divide that number by twelve and find what your monthly home-owning expense is. Then, if you are only considering your living arrangement as a necessary expense rather than as an investment, the elaborate formula we have just led you through will let you know whether it is cheaper for you to own or rent.

Now, let's consider home ownership as an investment. One thing to keep in mind is liquidity. Houses are not quickly converted into cash. When you decide to sell, your house could be on the market for months. Maybe it's overpriced. There could be a surplus of houses for sale, and few interested buyers. There is also the possibility that you will want to sell at a time when lending institutions are tightening up on available money. Your buyer might not be able to get a loan.

Generally, houses are invested in for the long-term gain. You need to consider the additional expenses incurred in the course of buying and selling. (Not to mention your own sanity which may be jeopardized by too many moves in too short a time!) Such expenses as escrow, real estate commissions, termite inspections (required in some states), and lender's fees must all be subtracted before true profit is realized.

You may live in an area of the country where there's a real estate boom. If you do, your house may earn more money just sitting there than you do going to work each day! This sort of market is the exception rather than the rule. There is no way of knowing whether the bonanza will continue, slow down, or come to a screeching halt. Optimists say it will go on forever. Pessimists think the bubble is about to burst. Real estate people are likely to tell you whatever is most likely to get you to buy or sell since it is in these transactions that they make their commissions.

Another factor to consider in home ownership is the interest rate on your loan. You may have bought at an opportune time when the interest rate was quite low. If you were to sell and re-invest right now, you might discover that interest rates are much higher. We cannot go into the elaborate pressure from the political and private sector that affects interest rates. Generally, if you discover that your interest rate is 8% or lower, you have excellent financing. If you are thinking of selling and re-investing, be sure to find out what the lenders are currently asking. You may be in for a shock! While rates of interest have varied dramatically in recent years, even a new low is not likely to compare favorably with the interest rates of yesteryear.

A term which is frequently bandied around in real estate circles is *leverage*. If you have taken physics, you may remember experiments where pulleys were used to increase your ability to lift something. Or perhaps you recall in your youth arranging your position on a teeter-totter so you could lift a bigger person. That is leverage. In real estate investment terms, leverage is making a small amount of money reap a big profit. It works on the concept that your house or other property will sell for more than you paid for it and that you borrow most of the money to buy it with.

We will use a highly unlikely example to simplify this concept of leverage. Suppose you found a house that you wanted to buy as an investment. The house costs $100,000. You put down $20,000 and get a loan for $80,000. The very next day, a buyer comes along and offers you $120,000 for the house (we told you this was a highly unlikely example!) Of course, you immediately sell the house. Wasn't that marvelous? You just made a $20,000 profit.

Now, here comes the question which will explain the concept of real estate leverage. What *percentage* of profit did you make on your investment? Before you pull out your pocket calculator and try to figure out whether to divide $120,000 into $100,0000, or vice versa, stop and think. *You* only put $20,000 into that house. The lender put in the rest. When you sell the house, you pay back the $80,000 loan but nothing more. The lender does not share any of the profit. You have invested $20,000 and wind up with $40,000. Therefore you made a 100% return on your investment! Most investments you make will never pay off this swiftly or lucratively. But it does get you excited about the concept of leverage, doesn't it?

Before you get too excited about the $20,000 you just made in one day, remember your relative in the nation's capital. There's Uncle Sam, with his hand out! You have just made a short-term capital gain, which will show up like regular income when tax time rolls around. If you had waited a year, you would still pay a capital gains tax but the gain would be considered long-term. Taxes on long-term capital gains are a little less severe.

There is also one more alternative. You could reinvest your money in the same or higher-priced property. If you do this, your capital gains tax will be postponed. Some people just keep selling and reinvesting in this fashion until they die.

Then the capital gains tax is taken out of their estate in the form of federal estate tax.

You may wonder whether you will find something you want at the same or a higher price than what you sold. The present economic situation of spiraling inflation seems bound to continue. New home construction has continued at near-boom proportions. Incomes have generally kept pace with prices. And demand is high. Shortages of skilled labor and materials such as lumber, cement, wallboard, and insulation are pushing costs up. In addition, the postwar baby boom "babies" are now adults buying homes for growing families of their own. There is a dramatic upswing in divorces. This means more separate households. Single people and unmarried couples who previously might have rented are now buying homes, too. The fact that interest rates are high and people are still buying is an indicator that "real estate mania" seems to have taken hold.

The dramatic rise in real estate values over the last decade may have begun to worry you. Can homes really be worth what they are selling for? If you invest now, can you depend on being able to find a buyer for your property at a higher price than you paid for it? (This is known in real estate as the "greater fool" theory.) As long as inflation is strong, prices of new and existing single-family dwellings should go up more than the cost of living.

At this point, you may be asking yourself, "If real estate is so good, why should I even consider other investments?" So far we have been talking just about the single-family housing market. It's the easiest market to judge because that is the type of property commonly owned and on which we have good price data. Actually, *investment* real estate went through a serious depression in 1974 and 1975 while prices of single-family homes were still increasing. There was a tremendous over-expansion in construction of income properties such as hotels, office buildings, and shopping centers. Many of these properties dropped in value. Some actually went broke.

If you've made the decision to own your own home and want to proceed further in investment properties, a good place to begin is with another single-family residence that you can rent out. "Blood, sweat and tears" real estate would probably be your safest speculation. Look for a house in a good location that is somewhat rundown. Invest some time and money fixing it up yourself. Look for retired carpenters, plumbers, et al, in your city who would be happy to work under your close supervision. When the house is fixed up, raise the rent or put it back on the market at a higher price. You may not make a fortune overnight, nor will it be easy, but your rental property should appreciate in value because you have done something that merits an increase in selling price.

Buying a home is no easy task. Be very cautious about the advice you receive from real estate sales people and well-meaning friends. In some states an attorney is needed to transfer title to real property. In other states, this is not true. Whatever the case in your state, we believe it's money well spent to have a real estate attorney review all papers before you commit yourself to any contracts. This probably will not be the same attorney you used for your divorce or probate proceedings.

Co-operative Apartment versus Condominium

There are other alternatives to owning a house. Cooperative apartments and condominiums have become very popular in recent years. They offer many of the advantages of owning a home without any of the burdens. Let's analyze each of these alternatives.

In a co-op apartment, a corporation builds or buys a building, then sells shares together with a proprietary lease to each tenant. Basically, this means that you, the tenant, do not actually own your own apartment. Instead, you are a shareholder, holding stock in the corporation which owns the building. You are also a lessee. Financially, you are responsible for paying your share of the costs of operation, maintenance, repairs, insurance, mortgage, taxes and any other assessment necessary to keep the building in order. You decorate and maintain your own apartment.

Cooperative apartment owners get the same tax advantage as homeowners. Your share of the co-op's mortgage interest and real estate taxes is deductible on your income tax. The part of your payment which pays off the co-op's loan increases your equity in the building.

There are some other advantages, too. You may be delighted to find that you are not personally responsible for building maintenance or repairs. These are usually taken care of by a manager or management firm. Also, you are not personally liable for the mortgage. On the other hand, these advantages can be disadvantages. Often you can't make major alterations in your apartment without approval of the co-op's board of directors. You probably can't sell or assign your apartment without approval of the co-op's board of directors. It may be less threatening to you not to be financially liable for the mortgage. But because of this arrangement, you can't use the equity you have built up as collateral for a loan. (You can do this with a home or a condominium.) Another liability is your fellow tenants (shareholders). If one of them can't meet her carrying charges (many of which are not fixed), she will have to sell, sublease, or surrender her stock. This places a serious burden on the rest of you since your assessments will increase to pick up the tab for the defaulting tenant until a new one can be found.

Condominium ownership has certain advantages over the co-op, plus some of the carefree maintenance features. You actually own your own apartment. You are taxed on it as a separate entity. You can mortgage it and borrow on your equity. This means an important source of ready cash. You also own the common parts of the project (halls, gardens, recreation facilities, etc.) jointly with other owners and pay your proportionate share for maintaining these facilities. As a condo owner, you are responsible for the taxes and mortgage on your own apartment. If any other owner defaults on his mortgage, the holder of that mortgage, usually a lending institution, can foreclose. But you and the rest of the owners are not substantially affected. As in co-ops, you can't expect to make radical decorative changes without the approval of the board of directors.

Savings and loans and other lending institutions are more inclined to lend you money for a condominium than a co-operative apartment since each condominium is treated as a private home rather than a share in a corporation. We feel condo ownership is the best alternative to owning a house. Of course, your decision must be based on many things, including the state of the economy, mortgage money available to you, and your own personal preferences.

Investing in Apartments

Most of us have lived in an apartment at one time or another in our lives. Some of you may even have helped the landlord from time to time by collecting rent, keeping books, or showing vacant apartments. You probably did this in exchange for a reduction in your rent. Have you ever imagined yourself as the *owner?*

Owning an apartment building is an active rather than a passive real estate investment. If you've lived in an apartment, you know that toilets clog, tenants have wild parties, garbage disposals break, people lock themselves out in the middle of the night or try to hide forbidden pets, and there's one in every crowd who will *never* pay the rent on time! Whether or not you employ a manager to run things for you, the ultimate responsibility is yours. It can be a really exciting career. But you should know yourself and your temperament and be willing to spend time as well as money on your investment.

Before you consider investing in an apartment complex, you should carefully and personally inspect the property. What kind of condition is it in? What is required in the way of maintenance? Talk to realtors about the neighborhood. Is

119

it static, improving or deteriorating? What is the vacancy factor in the complex? In comparable complexes? What percent vacancy can you handle and still make a profit? What are the taxes on the property? Are they increasing? Is a resident manager necessary? Apartment complexes can range from a duplex to a thousand units or more with swimming pools and recreational facilities.

You should examine the last three years' income tax returns on the property. This should give you a good idea if the seller is giving you valid information.

In financing, you may want to consider two alternatives. If you make a small down payment, your loan will be relatively large. The theory of leverage will work to your advantage. But most of the money you collect from renters will probably go to make the payments on your loan.

On the other hand, if you make a large down payment, you'll have less leverage but more income. Your loan and loan payments will be smaller. After you pay your lender each month, there will be more money left over for you.

As an investment, there are four major advantages to owning apartments.

1. Tax-sheltered income (you can claim depreciation and loan interest on your income tax).

2. Appreciation of property in general.

3. You can build up equity as you pay off your loan.

4. You can use leverage to make the most from any appreciation of your property.

The major disadvantage is that you are responsible for the management of the property. If you employ someone to manage it for you, this will decrease your monthly net income. You also have the problem of liquidity which accompanies all real estate investments. And there is the risk of obsolescence. The property may go down in value through no fault of yours or the manager. The neighborhood may change for the worse and leave you with a vacancy problem.

Buying apartments is a large commitment of your time and money. It can be lucrative if you buy at the right time for the right price. Always keep one thing in mind though. "Do i really want to be a landlord?"

Undeveloped Real Estate

Almost every major American city has an area that a few years ago was a scenic area, or perhaps was the unofficial city dump, which today is the site of shopping centers, tourist and entertainment facilities and valuable residential property. The original owners of the scenic farmlands or even the untended vacant dumps probably made fortunes when they sold their land to developers.

Undeveloped real estate is unimproved, or "raw" land. It is a risky investment but one which can offer high rewards if the timing and price are right.

The only tax savings you get from investing in vacant land are deductions for mortgage interest and taxes. Unlike real estate, raw land is not a depreciable asset. You do not get the tax benefit of depreciation that would apply to a house or apartment building. Your investment is based on the hope that the land will increase in value.

What should you look for in buying a piece of vacant land? Look for patterns of living and movement of people to find favorable locations. As the boundaries of suburbia widen, what was once open country becomes a part of the metropolitan sprawl.

Much of the population of this country has been moving to the West and Southwest sections of the United States. The "Sunbelt" is a new term describing these areas. In addition, there is still some potentially valuable vacant land in the Northeast and other heavily developed areas.

Vacation areas are steadily growing due to increased leisure time. The rising popularity of a certain sport, like skiing, can make land in what was once desolate areas valuable property. Taxes may be low since the community does not have to provide many public services. Low taxes can give the investor more time to hold the land. This time factor may be critical. You need to sell at the right time to make a profit.

121

Alone

When it comes time to sell, you will want a team of professionals on your side. For example, you may find you can realize a larger profit if you subdivide the land and sell it in individual lots, instead of one large parcel. This may take more money, but your profit might be treated as ordinary income. The Internal Revenue Service might claim that by subdividing and selling, you have put yourself into the business of real estate. You then have your profits taxed as ordinary income, rather than capital gains. There are ways to avoid this, but you need the help of a real estate tax expert. Do not try to cut corners by doing it yourself.

Improved Real Estate

Remember playing "Monopoly" when you were a youngster? Your first few times around the board, you bought every piece of property you landed on. The players who landed on your squares paid you a little rent but not much. Then the game got livelier. You tried to own *all* the property of a certain color. You crossed your fingers and prayed while you rolled the dice. Or you made shrewd and crafty deals with other players. When you owned all the property of the same color, you could start to "build." One house increased the rent dramatically. Four houses or a hotel wiped the other player out!

Obviously, real life isn't just like Monopoly. But owning a piece of land with something on it can be very profitable. Improved real estate means "land plus improvements." "Improvements" can be anything from a small parking lot to an office complex or major shopping center.

You will probably want to use leverage for this kind of investment. We've talked about leverage before but the concept is not an easy one to grasp and it bears repeating. Suppose you buy a duplex for $100,000. You put down $40,000 in cash and obtain a mortgage or trust deed for the rest, which is $60,000. Then you decide to sell for $125,000. That $25,000 profit belongs to you. You have made a 60% return

122

on your original $40,000 investment. This profit is made possible by leverage with the use of a mortgage.

Mortgage financing also gives you tax savings. The interest you pay your lender is tax deductible. Tax allowances for depreciation can also be an important advantage. Your depreciation is based on the entire market value, not just on your equity.

Depending on the nature of the investment, there can be a minor or major leasing, rental and mangement problem. You will want expert advice before committing yourself to this type of investment.

Real Estate Investment Advice

Certain emotions are so common to the buying and selling of real estate that you have probably already heard of them. You may even have experienced them personally. Horrible feelings sweep over you the minute you sign on the dotted line! "Did I buy too quickly? Is it really a lemon?" "Did I sell too quickly? Was it really a plum?"

You are suffering from buyer's (or seller's) remorse. Generally, you have an overwhelming conviction that you have made a big mistake and now it is too late to get out of it!

The best preventive measure for these unpleasant feelings of remorse is reliable real estate advice. Investment counselors, bank trust departments and investment letters abound with advice for the securities market. Such advice seems sparse in the real estate field. Where do you go for help?

The person most available to you is a real estate broker. A broker with a well-established reputation will probably be well-informed. She can be very helpful. But you must remember that, like a stockbroker, she is not a disinterested party. She makes her living selling real property. Once you've found something you like, have an attorney who specializes in real estate law advise you before you sign any documents. There should be no place for remorse in your life!

Trust Deeds:
An Income Investment Secured by Real Estate

Have you ever picked your way through the racks of skirts or blouses in a discount factory outlet looking for loose seams or invisible flaws? You'll find some really great bargains! "Seconds" in the real estate market can be just as attractive.

Second trust deeds (or mortgages) are called that because they are junior in lien to the first trust deed (or mortgage) on a piece of property. To oversimplify slightly, this means that if a property is foreclosed, the holder of the first trust deed will be paid off first, and then the holder of the second trust deed. We'll talk more about foreclosure later in this section.

Notes secured by second deeds of trust, which are similar to second mortgages in some states, have become increasingly popular investments in areas which are experiencing a real estate boom. Soaring home values in these areas of the country permit homeowners to cash in on their increased equity by borrowing on that equity with the use of "seconds." Many homeowners do so by borrowing from banks, savings and loans, or finance companies. Or they can use a private lender.

Private mortgage loan-brokers match homeowners who want to borrow with individuals who have money to lend. They do this for a fee.

As a "private lender" or "investor," you will find that seconds are reasonably safe. They offer a ten percent or more return on your money. The borrower is the one who pays the broker's fee. In most cases, there are no fees or commissions charged to the investor. This is something to remember when you are calculating your net return on an investment.

Second trust deeds, themselves, are nothing new. They go back almost as far as real estate debt. But only recently have they become popular as an investment for the private individual. Some investors are using seconds as an alternative to such conservative investments as utility stocks and corporate bonds. Others are using them for pension fund money such as Keogh Plans and Individual Retirement Accounts (we will talk about these later in this chapter).

State laws controlling foreclosure proceedings and interest rate limitations determine whether seconds are popular in your state.

We've come a long way from the days when the dastardly villain in the black cape twirled his mustache and sneered gleefully as he drove poor Dudley DoRight and his devoted wife from their modest home because they missed a mortgage payment! Taking back title to real property for default in payment is a lengthy and complicated legal proceeding, designed to protect the vested interest of the homeowner. In some states, especially where second mortgages prevail, foreclosure is difficult and may require two or three trips to court over a two or three-year period. Investigate the foreclosure procedure in your state. If foreclosure is exceptionally difficult, seconds are not an investment we would recommend. Your alternative is to invest your money in another state.

Interest rates on seconds are also determinative. For example, New York is limited to lower interest rates than California or Arizona. Michigan allows only a 7% interest rate while Massachusetts allows up to 18%. Penalties for charging too much interest can range from a small fine to a stay in jail.

A quick way to find out what's happening in your state is to check the media. Do you hear seconds mentioned on the radio or television? Do you see ads in the newspaper? If not, there's probably a fly in the ointment. Seconds are not popular in your state and for good reason.

At the end of this chapter is a list you can check for your state's interest rate and foreclosure procedures. Some states have both mortgages and trust deeds. We have listed the form which is most often used. A few states have their own formula to calculate maximum interest. In those cases, we have stated "formula."

For detailed information about formula calculations, maximum interest or foreclosure proceedings, contact your attorney or your state Real Estate Commissioner. If you live in a major city, the phone number and address of the Real Estate Commissioner will be listed in your local directory.

When the majority of financial periodicals address themselves to the second trust deed market, they usually zero in on California. Buying a second trust deed in California is a relatively simply procedure. First interview and investigate the credentials of several mortgage brokers. Choose one and tell her how much money you would like to invest. Three thousand dollars is usually the minimum.

Your broker will give you a loan package to study. Make sure that the amount of money you are investing in the second trust deed plus the money secured by the first trust deed is less than 80% of the appraised value of the property. Corroborate the amount of the first trust deed loan. Have the first trust deed payments been regular and prompt? Establish that the appriased value is reasonable. Was the property appraised by a licensed real estate appraiser? If the property is in your city, take the time to look at it. Remember, the property will be your security for the loan.

If the loan package seems too complicated for you the first time around, ask for help from your banker. He won't charge you and should be happy to help.

When you find a loan you like, turn your money over to your mortagage broker. When she has recorded your newly-acquired second trust deed with the county recorder's office, you'll receive a package of loan documents. You may again want to review these with your banker. After your first investment, the others will follow the same formula and seem easier to you.

After all the paper work is finished, you should receive a regular monthly check according to the terms of your loan. It is customary for the borrower to pay the broker, who forwards the payments to you. It is also customary that the broker deal with delinquent debtors. Again, remember that your security is the real estate. Your position is subordinate to that of the first trust deed lender. In practice, borrowers who get in trouble usually sell their houses. The proceeds are used to pay off the first and second trust deed holders.

With people constantly on the move, prepayment penalties

aren't uncommon. A prepayment penalty is an added percentage paid the lender if the borrower elects to pay off the note ahead of schedule. Since people often sell their homes and pay off their loans, this can greatly increase your yield. The length of the loan can range from one to seven years or more. We suggest you invest for as short a time as possible. With inflation, interest rates, and the law constantly being changed, you don't want to get locked into a relatively low interest rate.

What are the disadvantages of second trust deeds? The income is fully taxable for one. For another, if the real estate market dropped 20 percent or more you could lose part or all of your principal since the owner of the first trust deed is paid off before you. Also, you have committed your money and while it is possible for you to sell your trust deed, the investment is not liquid. To sell quickly you might have to take a loss. Notes secured by second trust deeds can be a good conservative investment for you if you do your homework before taking the plunge.

Taxation and Investments

In this section, you get some good news and some bad news. The good news is, with some of your investments, you may be lucky enough to make a "killing." The bad news is, you have a silent partner, Uncle Sam.

Shocking but true, Uncle Sam can take up to seventy percent of your profit. Some of you will think it's "bad news" just to have to read about taxes. Before you (yawn!) close your eyes. . .or the book. . .we want to give you a little positive reinforcement.

Understanding some of the fundamentals of taxation is absolutely critical if you're going to succeed as an investor. "I can't figure all that stuff out" is a sentence many women save for anything that has to do with numbers. This feeling of frustration and hopelessness that makes you want to give up even before you start is so common there's even a name for it, "math anxiety." You may have a similar mental block at this point in the section.

"I can't understand all that stuff" is not an acceptable excuse to quit now. You're not fooling us. We know you can!

Take a break if you need to. Get a fresh cup of hot coffee, milk and an apple, or take a walk around the block. Come back with the positive mental attitude that you want to and can understand all you need to know about taxes to become a smart investor. When you get back, begin

HERE:

There are two basic things you need to know about income taxation. Simply stated, it's the difference between "ordinary income" and "capital gains and capital losses."

Ordinary income is the most common kind of income, the money you make on your job. Graduated ordinary income tax rates are applied to it. Income you receive from your investments, such as dividends, rents and interest, is added to the rest of your ordinary income and this graduated tax still applies, with just a few exceptions. Interest from municipal bonds is excluded. There is also an exemption (for the first $100) for dividends paid to investors by US corporations.

Capital Gains and Losses. When a capital asset is sold, the profit, if any, is treated as a capital gain. Most investments you make outside a business will come within the capital asset category. Stocks, bonds, real estate, gold, silver diamonds, are all examples of capital assets. Types of properties which do not qualify are notes and accounts receivable acquired in the course of doing business, copyrights and other artistic properties, and certain government obligations issued at a discount. When you sell a capital asset, the tax is on the difference between what you originally paid for the asset and the price at which you sell. If the sale price is more, you have a gain. If the sale price is less, then you have a loss for your income tax.

Uncle Sam is also interested in the length of time separating your transactions of buying and selling. If you hold an asset for one year or less and then sell it, you have realized a *short-term* capital gain or loss. If it is a gain, it gets taxed as ordinary income.

If you hold an asset for one year or longer, it is taxed as a *long-term* capital gain. This means that 50% of your gain is added to your gross income for that year and taxed as ordinary income. For example, if you have a $10,000 long-term capital gain and you are in a 20% ordinary income tax bracket, then you would pay 20% on $5,000 (which is 50% of your capital gain). Many taxpayers have the common belief that long-term capital gains under $50,000 are taxed at a flat 25% rate. As you can see from the above example, this is untrue. Many people have overpaid their tax due to this misconception.

In this "win-a-few, lose-a-few" investment world, it is likely that you may have both gains and losses in the same year. If there is a capital loss, be it short or long-term, it is first deducted against any gains. But if the short-term losses exceed the gains in any one year, then you can deduct up to $3,000 of the excess from your ordinary income. If it's a long-term loss, then only 50% of it can be used to offset ordinary income up to the same $3,000 maximum. Any loss left over after this deduction can be carried forward as a short or long-term capital loss, using the same rules, until it is used up. No one likes losses. But you can't just ignore them! Sell that old "penny stock" that was going to make you rich. Using your losses can put real tax dollars back into your pocket. That's what we mean by the "bottom line."

Now that you know a little bit more about taxes (aren't you proud of yourself?), let's talk about some more sophisticated investments.

Tax Shelters

As a suddenly single woman, you've been out of circulation for awhile. Dating takes some getting used to if you were a teenager the last time you tried. You may find that your social skills need a little brushing up. We're here to help!

Let's picture you at a table for two. The lights are low. The drinks have been served. Your date seems very nice. But the conversation has been a bit slow. Now there's an awkward pause. Your date lines his fork up a little straighter on the linen napkin. You gaze admiringly at the chandelier. He clears his throat, suave devil that he is, and asks cleverly, "Have you seen any good movies lately?" You lower your eyes slowly from the chandelier, meet his eager gaze, and reply demurely, "Why, no. But I've heard of some great tax shelters." With that line and the rest of this section behind you, you have enough scintillating material to last at least through dessert and an after-dinner drink!

People love to talk about tax shelters. There's a lot of sparkle to it. You may find yourself picturing a suede shoe artist peddling the latest "loophole." You, too, it seems, can get "one-up" on Uncle Sam.

Actually, there are many misconceptions about tax shelters. They are not "loopholes" and they are not used just by the rich. Some tax sheltering may be valuable for you to reach your financial goals. Picture a rainy day situation. Sometimes you would rush under a shelter until the rain let up, while other times you might just settle for getting wet.

We feel that the first tax shelter you should consider is a conservative one that you may use if you are self-employed. You can picture this as an umbrella against taxes.

There are roughly ten million people in the United States who are self-employed. If you own or start a small business, this puts you in the ranks of the self-employed.

There are no ready-made pension or profit sharing plans for the self-employed. Our tax laws were set up to benefit the employee, the woman who works for someone else. Due to some tax changes in recent years, the self-employed woman can take the initiative and provide for her own retirement.

In this section we will discuss Individual Retirement Accounts, Keogh Plans, and profit sharing plans available under the Employee Retirement Income Security Act of 1974 (ERISA).

Individual Retirement Accounts

Your employer may not have established a qualified retirement plan for you or you may have chosen not to participate in one. If so, you may establish your own Individual Retirement Account (IRA).

You may invest up to $1,500 or 15% of your annual compensation (whichever is smaller) in an IRA each year. A married employee with a nonworking spouse can establish a joint IRA. Contributions are limited to the lesser of $1,750 or 15% of compensation. If both spouses work, each can establish an IRA. The $1,500/15% limitation applies to each. All interest and appreciation in an IRA accumulate tax free. No withdrawals are permitted before age fifty-nine and a half. Withdrawals must begin by age seventy and a half. Withdrawals are taxed as ordinary income (at the theoretically lower post-retirement tax rate).

There are many investment vehicles for IRA plans. They include trust and custody accounts which can be invested in savings accounts, retirement annuities, endowment contracts, mutual funds, and securities.

Keogh Plans

If you're self-employed, depending on your income level, a Keogh Plan might be for you. Under this plan you set aside between $750 and $7,500 each year tax free for your retirement. Your money has to be placed into a bank trust department or independent trust company. You may then choose how you want the money invested for you.

Contributions to a Keogh Plan may be invested in a variety of ways: stocks, bonds, mutual funds, second trust deed, etc. All growth and income accumulate tax free. After retirement, you pay tax on the money as you withdraw it from the plan.

The Keogh Act is not a simple one to explain. We'll do our best with a relatively simple example. If you qualify, you'll want to get down to the nitty-gritty of this plan with your tax advisor.

Dr. Smith is a successful surgeon. She is in the 50% tax bracket. She makes $75,000 per year. She decides to set up a Keogh Plan. She can now put away 15% of her income (in this case 15% of $75,000 or $11,500) *or* $7,500 whichever is *less*. The entire contribution is tax deductible. This means that if she puts in the maximum allowed, $7,500, she has saved $3,750 in taxes.

Dr. Smith's money accumulates free of both capital gains and income tax. Because Dr. Smith is in the 50% tax bracket, her contribution can gain twice as much because it is not taxed at this point. When Dr. Smith qualifies for retirement, she is taxed at preferential rates.

Pension and Profit Sharing Plans

Since enactment of the Employee Retirement Income Security Act of 1974 (ERISA), professionals (doctors, lawyers, accountants, architects, etc.) who incorporate themselves can set up profit sharing plans. The "corporation" can then contribute up to 15% of the annual compensation paid each participant (which contribution is limited, however, to a maximum of $25,000) to a profit sharing plan and trust. The contribution by the corporation is deductible in computing corporate income tax. At the same time, the contribution made on behalf of each employee is not currently taxed to the employee. Rather, the taxation is "deferred" until the employee withdraws his account balances from the plan. Incorporated professionals may also establish pension plan contributions which are tax deductible. As in Keogh Plans, all growth and income accumulate tax free.

The Why of Tax Shelters

We have just given you three examples of tax shelters. IRA's, Keogh Plans, and profit sharing plans for professionals under ERISA, are each designed to encourage the self-employed to provide for retirement. In plain English, Uncle Sam doesn't want a lot of penniless old people around who are dependent on the state when they're too old to work. Like dangling the carrot before the donkey, Uncle Sam encourages planned provision for retirement by offering an incentive. The incentive is tax-sheltered income during the earning years.

Tax shelters are better understood when you look at them as "incentives" rather than "loopholes." As we discuss real estate, oil and gas exploration, equipment leasing and agricultural tax shelters, consider the "whys" as well as the "wherefores" of these investment opportunities

Real Estate Tax Shelters

Uncle Sam thinks it would be a great country if we all owned our own homes. He's a great promoter of real estate development. It comes as no surprise, then, that real estate is undoubtedly the most popular tax shelter. Many real estate shelters are very complicated. We'll give you an idea of what some of them are all about.

Tax sheltered real estate investments are usually arranged in the form of limited partnerships. A limited partnership is an investment project between an individual and/or company (the general partner) and a group of investors. The general partner has investment expertise and the group of investors (called limited partners) seek specific tax benefits, risks and rewards. The profits from limited partnerships are shared according to a stated formula designed to compensate the general partner and the investors for their respective contributions. As an investor, you will have many tax advantages. In addition, your personal liability is legally limited to only the amount of money you've actually invested. The general partner has liability for all other losses incurred.

Real estate limited partnerships involve undeveloped land, office buildings, apartments, industrial parks, shopping centers, mobile home parks and more.

Now we will describe some specific investments.

Newly constructed real estate partnerships construct new buildings or purchase new "first user" buildings. Typically, such partnerships involve maximum *leverage* and employ *accelerated depreciation*. The accounting theory of depreciation is based on the expectation that sooner or later everything wears out. In accounting, many buildings are considered to wear out or depreciate over a twenty-five year period. In real life, we know some fifty-year-old structures are in better condition than some five-year-old buildings. Understanding the theory of depreciation and using it to your advantage requires some sophistication on your part as an investor (and taxpayer). We encourage you to discuss the depreciation terms we use in this section with your real estate tax advisor. Because of the more favorable *double declining balance* depreciation (at 200% of straight line depreciation rate), these programs usually concentrate on new apartment construction. Sometimes commercial developments (office buildings and shopping centers) are included for diversification. These are limited to 150% *declining balance* depreciation.

Existing Income Producing Real Estate. These partnerships usually invest in existing commercial properties and apartments. Because of slower depreciation methods and lower leverage, most existing property programs offer lower tax losses in early years (10% to 20% the first year) and significant opportunities for tax-sheltered cash flow. Hence the name, "income producing real estate." Lower leverage on existing (and therefore more predictable) rental properties implies lesser risk.

Net Leased Real Estate. These partnerships purchase office buildings, hotels, shopping centers, factory buildings, warehouses, etc., on a leveraged basis. Properties are leased to major corporations on a long term, "triple net lease" basis. In a triple net lease, the corporate tenant is responsible for a specified lease payment plus all taxes, insurance, maintenance and other expenses.

Tax losses the first year are minimal. Remember, tenants pay operating costs. The partnership's only deductions are interest and straight-line depreciation. The real benefit in a net lease situation is the opportunity for a relatively low-risk investment yielding cash flow. Furthermore, this money is partially sheltered from tax depreciation. Usually about 50 % of the cash received over the life of the partnership is tax-sheltered.

Government Assisted Housing. These investments involve construction or rehabilitation of properties for low income, middle income, or elderly tenants. They offer good investment opportunities for women needing to shelter income. But since they depend upon funding from various state and federal housing finance programs, they are not always available.

Oil and Gas. Since the recent embargo, oil companies have been sending darling little dinosaurs into our living rooms at night to tell us how difficult it is to find oil. Oil and gas accumulate in the pore space of underground rock formations. A given "reservoir," as these accumulations are called, may be small or may contain millions of barrels of oil or billions of cubic feet of natural gas. They can also turn out to be "dry holes."

Because of high costs and risks, oil and gas companies are often forced to seek outside cash to finance drilling. Individual investors supply much of the industries' drilling capital through tax shelter limited partnerships. Uncle Sam is all in favor of finding new sources of oil and gas. So we are given an incentive. Oil and gas partnerships offer opportunities for high first year tax losses. They are also the riskiest tax shelter because of the possibility of dry holes.

Equipment Leasing. Did you ever have the secret urge to operate a fork lift or a bulldozer? Do you grab at chances to tour factories? Are you curious about how steel is produced, land is cleared, livestock is transported, or how rubber is turned into airplane wheels? Heavy industry makes America run. But many of us never come very close to it in our daily lives. An equipment leasing partnership could be a vicarious outlet for your curiosity.

Virtually any industrial equipment can be leased: airplanes, computers, trucks, drilling rigs, railroad cars and even entire factories. Equipment leasing partnerships require the following "ingredients":

1. Investors to provide equity capital.
2. Sponsors to supervise partnership operations.
3. Lenders (banks or insurance companies) to provide loans.
4. User.
5. Leasable equipment.

Equipment leasing is a low-risk tax shelter but it is not riskless. Uncle Sam wouldn't have to coax you into it if there were no problems! The risk of user failure is always present. Even companies with top credit ratings sometimes can't meet their obligations.

Agriculture. Now here's an investment for you city slickers with a secret desire to get back to the basics. What could be more basic than food and lumber? Agricultural tax shelters include partnerships for investment in cattle feeding, cattle and other livestock breeding, crops and timber. You may feel emotionally "turned off" at the idea of cutting down trees. If you have a sort of "Woodsman, spare that tree!" attitude, remember, they always plant more.

How Do I Choose?

When you consider all these investment possibilities, you may feel overwhelmed. If you're interested, start by considering the ones that you feel you can relate to. Then learn everything about them. Analyzing any of these tax shelters requires in-depth knowledge of partnership law, taxation, the industry and the general partner's management and operations. We suggest you rely on a tax expert when you arrive at this stage of investing.

Savings Institutions

As we have mentioned previously in this chapter, a savings account is not good as an investment, but it is both good and necessary for your financial flexibility and stability. In your savings account, your money has no protection against inflation and taxes and no opportunity for appreciation of capital. There is, however, a guaranteed rate of return. Besides this, short-term savings accounts also offer liquidity.

Most savings accounts are insured either by the Federal Savings and Loan Insurance Corporation or by the Federal Deposit Insurance Corporation. Except for federal savings and loan associations which are required to carry Federal Savings and Loan Insurance Corporation insurance, the insurance need not be provided by a federal agency. The insurance on your account could be private. That little known fact should shock you. As a matter of fact, recently an "insured" bank turned out to be insured by a private insurance company whose office was a store in Algeria! So, depositors, check carefully on the type of insurance your savings institution carries.

You may, until now, have vaguely lumped all savings institutions together. Let's take a careful look at various types of savings institutions. Some of the information you learn here will not only surprise you but should benefit you.

Savings and Loan Associations

Savings and loans specialize in home financing. They may pay a higher return than other major savings institutions. This is because home mortgages can earn a greater return than government securities, so savings and loans may have larger earnings to distribute. Savings and loans operate under either state or federal charters with close government regulation.

Mutual Savings Bank

Mutual savings banks are chartered by the state in which they operate. State laws limit their investments in mortgages to about 65% of assets. The rest of Mutual Savings Banks' assets go into conservative corporate bonds, government securities and a few common stocks.

137

Commercial Banks

The interest rates on savings accounts at commercial banks are usually lower than other savings institutions. This is because the Federal Reserve Bank limits maximum interest rates they may pay with respect to certain time deposits. Commercial banks' interest rates usually run about one quarter of a per cent lower than other savings institutions.

Credit Unions

Any group of people who have a common interest, for example, teachers, may form a credit union. Credit unions are state or federally chartered. The group pools its savings and makes these savings available for loans to its members. Because credit unions have low administrative costs and are tax exempt, they can pay higher interest rates. So what's the catch? Credit unions do not have the federal insurance, or, often, the degree of professional management which most banks and savings and loans do. This could mean a lesser degree of safety.

Obligations of the Federal Government

Have you ever wondered what the national debt is all about? It's simple. Just like you and me, Uncle Sam borrows, too. The US government borrows money from its citizens in much the same way individuals borrow money. The debt must be repaid at a defined time called the maturity date. There is a set interest rate. Similar to putting your money in savings accounts, investing in obligations of the federal government offers little or no chance for the appreciation of principal. But they are absolutely the safest and they are backed by the US government. There are two types: marketable and nonmarketable.

Marketable US Obligations. Marketable issues are in the form of Treasury bills, certificates, notes and bonds. They are traded in the general market place so their value may change daily. If they are held to maturity date, the investor will receive back his principal plus interest. We suggest you investigate Treasury bills, as they can be as short term as ninety days. On the other hand, government bonds may tie up your money for twenty years or more. As mentioned before, due to inflation and changing tax laws, we don't advocate tying up your money for long periods of time.

Flower bonds are a nickname used for certain marketable government securities which at the death of the bond holder can be turned in at face or par value ($1,000 per bond) for payment of federal estate taxes. These bonds pay a low interest rate so they are purchased at a discount.

We will give you an example. Suppose these "flower bonds" were purchased for the portfolio of an extremely ill person at $800 per bond. Subsequently, this person dies. At the time of death that bond purchased for $800 can add to the estate an asset which will be worth $1,000 for the purpose of payment of federal estate taxes. There are other tax consequences which have to be dealt with in using these bonds. Capital gains could come into play. Again we remind you, your tax advisor should be consulted before purchasing these bonds.

Nonmarketable US Obligations. The larger part of the nonmarketable debt of the federal government is made up of *Series E Savings Bonds.* They were bought by citizens in large numbers during World War II as a patriotic duty. These bonds receive a special tax treatment. You may report the interest income in a lump sum when you redeem them *or* report the income on your yearly tax as it accrues. Also, when they mature, you do not *have* to cash them in. If you just add onto them and do nothing, they will still accrue interest every six months. A procrastinator's dream! (But watch out for inflation.) Series E bonds have a minor restriction to discourage early redemption. No interest is paid for the first six months.

These bonds can be purchased for a face amount as little as $25 and a maximum of $10,000. They are popular gifts from grandparents.

Series H Savings Bonds are purchased by investors who want income now. They have no special tax treatment. They are sold in denominations starting at $500 with a maximum of $10,000. The interest which is paid every six months must be reported yearly. They have a 10-year maturity but they can be redeemed any time after six months from date of issue.

Both Series E's and H's have the ultimate safety of the US government behind them. The return is relatively low, fixed, and does not provide a hedge against inflation.

Municipal Bonds

Municipal bonds are debt obligations of states, local governments and authorities. The name "municipal" often confuses people because they may think of a municipality as a small town and might assume because of their name that most municipal bonds are offered by small communities. Bonds offered by the state of Texas, New York or California, bonds issued by the Illinois Turnpike (an "authority"), and school bonds issued by Tinytown, USA, are all examples of municipal bonds.

Why do people buy them? The interest from these bonds is tax free both federally and in the state where they are issued.

There are three principal types of municipal bonds:

General Obligation bonds are backed by the full faith and credit and general taxing power of the entity that issues them. Of the three types, they are usually the safest. It follows then, that they usually yield a lower return.

Revenue Bonds are issued for a specific purpose. A good example would be bonds issued to finance the Golden Gate Bridge in San Francisco. Bond holders are paid by revenues collected; in this case, by tolls collected on the bridge. The theory of revenue bonds is that the costs of a particular construction project should be borne by those who are going to use it.

Agency Bonds are issued for purposes of financing hospitals, university construction and state housing. These are basically revenue bonds but the state legislature is supposed to have a moral obligation to vote allocations for these projects if they do not generate sufficient income to support their own debt.

Municipal bonds are offered at a lower rate of return than corporate bonds because municipal bond interest is tax free. This may give you more spendable income if you are in a high tax bracket.

For example, take a taxpayer in the 60% income tax bracket. She buys a 5% tax free bond and gets a return equal to 12.5% in taxable interest. Now take the woman in a 25% bracket. She would get a return equal to 6.7% taxable interest. This is not a good investment for the second woman because she is taking a risk and could do as well in a savings and loan, which is insured.

What are the disadvantages of municipal bonds? Many of them are not as liquid as US government or corporate bonds. This is especially true if the entity that issued the bonds is small and not widely known. (New Yorkers are not interested in Tinytown's school bonds.) Municipal bonds should be thought of as long-term investments because bond prices fluctuate with interest rates.

Analyzing the credit rating of the issuing entity (municipal project or local government) is important. You need to be reasonably certain that your money will be paid back. Rating services such as Moody's and Standard & Poor's can be very helpful. At the end of this chapter you'll find a table explaining the comparative rating systems of these two services.

Even so, there can be surprises, like the one you got not too long ago if you were a "Big Apple" bondholder! Even the largest municipalities, like New York City, have their problems.

What you need to consider is whether your return on a particular municipal bond is substantially greater than the after-tax income you would receive on other types of investments.

Stocks

If you own stocks or are considering buying them, you're

concerned with investing in American industry. There are two different kinds of stock, common and preferred.

When you buy *common stock*, you own part of the company you've invested in. In theory, as the company prospers, the stock goes up in value and you get good quarterly dividends. Then you pat yourself on the back because you've made a wise investment. Unfortunately, it doesn't always work this way. Today's stock market has been influenced by economic problems such as inflation, the balance of trade and payments deficit and lack of confidence in the US dollar. But for now, let's put aside current economic trends and go back to the theory of stocks.

Stocks have the potential of being growth investments. They provide an opportunity for capital appreciation. The expectation of increased corporate profits provides the growth potential. Of course, it should not be forgotten that the potential for loss is also there. That is why stocks are more of a risk than bonds of the same company.

Common stocks tend to fall into two broad categories: blue chip stocks and growth stocks. For a corporation's stock to be considered blue chip, it must meet four very rigid standards.

1. The corporation must be a leader in American industry.

2. The corporation must have a proven record of earnings during good times *and* bad.

3. The company's record of dividend payments must be unbroken for a period of over twenty years.

4. There must be definite prospects for the company to continue this consistently good performance for the future.

Growth stocks are harder to define. You will never know if a stock fits into this category until after its growth is well underway. Hindsight is always 20/20! There are some characteristics growth stocks have in common.

First, the corporation must have adequate working capital. This money should be generated from within if possible. Second, the earnings should be compounding at an unusually high rate. Third, net income per share should be going up at approximately the same percentage as earnings. Fourth, the company must be a leader in the right industry at the right time.

People buy stocks for two reasons: dividends and the possibility of appreciation. Often the second reason is the most popular. Sometimes you can make a lot of money.

Another method of investing in American industry is through *preferred stock*. This type of stock gives you a limited ownership in the corporation with a higher and more secure dividend rate. The value of a preferred stock varies with interest rates as well as the performance of the company. You're taking less risk but getting less reward. You also give up some of the rights of a common stockholder for this extra stability, but you relinquish the ability to vote at annual stockholders' meetings.

There is a type of preferred stock which gives you more flexibility. It's called *convertible preferred*. This stock gives the owner the right to exchange her preferred stock for common stock in the same company under certain conditions.

As in all investments, there is a time to own convertible preferred and a time not to. The old cliche, "Buy low, sell high," won't work here. You must watch long-term interest rates. Avoid preferred stock in periods of rising long-term interest rates.

Bonds

There's a popular old song that begins "Love and marriage, love and marriage, go together like a horse and carriage." (If you're reading this recently divorced, you can still appreciate the rhyme!)

Stocks and bonds go together, too, like a horse and carriage. But, unlike the song, you *can* have one without the other.

When you buy a corporate bond, you make a loan to a corporation at a stated interest rate with your money to be paid back at a certain date in the future (maturity date). You are no longer an owner of a corporation. You are a creditor. You do not participate in any corporate profits.

Most bonds, called *debentures*, are backed only by the good name of the company to which you lend your money. Some bonds, however, are secured by a pledge or lien on the company's property or on specific assets. For example, a Railroad Equipment Bond is secured by a piece of railroad equipment.

As a bondholder, you have prior legal claim over both common and preferred stockholders with regard to both the assets of a corporation and its income. The interest on your bond will be paid before any of the stockholders get dividends.

What are the other advantages of corporate bonds? They yield more than government obligations. They provide a fixed rate of return. Repayment of the face amount is guaranteed by the corporation if you hold them to maturity. And, perhaps more important, there is usually an active bond market to insure liquidity.

The greatest disadvantage of bonds is their fixed interest rate. The bond market will decline in a time of rising interest rates. One way to hedge against this is to purchase *convertible bonds*. This type of bond gives you the right to convert to a certain number of shares of the common stock of the company. This offers the security of a fixed return investment as well as the growth opportunities of an "equity" or "ownership" investment.

Another disadvantage is that, except for convertibles, bonds have a potential for growth only if general interest rates decline. The safety of a bond is only as good as the company that issues it. The company must have the ability to continually pay interest and repay principal.

Mutual Funds

Like Twiggy and the Beatles, white boots and "mod" miniskirts, mutual funds were the rage of the sixties. A mutual fund is a pool of money contributed by a group of people. The money is invested for them by specialists in a variety of stocks and/or bonds. Mutual funds are directed toward a specific investment goal: growth, growth with income, or just income.

If you have money invested in a mutual fund, you probably aren't too happy with it now. Mutual funds haven't done very well in the last ten years. This decade has been a rough one for the stock market and mutual funds follow the same trend. In addition, many of them grew to be so large in the 1960's that they couldn't make the fast changes necessary for smart investing in the 1970's.

We've painted a pretty dismal picture. This picture could change radically if we were to have a bullish stockmarket. Who knows? The mini-skirt may rise again!

The Investment Counselor

"Whodunnits" make great leisure reading. But mysteries don't belong in your investment world. If you're excited about investing in stocks or bonds but somewhat confused, there are licensed professionals to help you.

A licensed investment counselor can give you the advantage of individualized service. In addition, her advice should be completely objective. She has nothing to sell but her services. An investment counselor is paid a percentage of the money she invests for you. It's to her advantage to make your estate grow. Naturally, there are no guarantees. You can still lose money. But your odds are a lot better than trying to do it for yourself.

You have to have a sizeable amount of money before an investment counselor will take you as a client. The minimum is usually $50,000. On this amount, you will pay a fee of from ½% to 2%. The percentage goes down as the amount of money increases. There is also consideration given for a smaller percentage fee when a portfolio requires less professional supervision.

If you don't have this kind of money, but still have some stocks and bonds (or want to invest in some), don't give up. We have some other ideas for you.

The Trust Department of Your Bank

All major banks and most community banks have trust departments which will handle stock and bond portfolios. Sometimes they will handle portfolios of less than $50,000. The only way to find out is to call some banks in your community and ask.

While you're on the phone, make an appointment with one of the bank's trust officers. No matter how little money you have, the trust officer can give you practical advice. And he doesn't charge for information.

Basically, trust departments have the preservation of an estate as their objective. The trust may come as the result of an inheritance. On the other hand, you may have created a trust and are considering a bank to assume management responsibilities.

Ask to see the results of the trust department's investment portfolio for common trust funds. The results of the last ten years should give you a good idea of how that particular trust department handles money.

Fees charged by bank trust departments tend to be about the same as those charged by private investment counselors; that is, ½% to 2%.

Stockbrokers

When you deal with a firm which is a member of the New York Stock Exchange, you will deal with a person who acts as its representative. She is known as a stockbroker.

What are her qualifications? She must have passed an exam given by the New York Stock Exchange and she must be registered with the Exchange. What does this say about the advice you'll get from her? Not much. She is provided with information researched by her company. She then tries to adapt that knowledge to your individual needs. Her success often depends more on the state of the economy than her willingness to help you. Investment advice cannot be guaranteed by examinations or formal registration. Also remember that your stockbroker makes a commission each time you buy and sell. She has a personal stake in dealing with you that could impair her objectivity.

No Fee Advisors

No Fee Advisors, often called "financial planners," make up the majority of advisors available to help you. Nobody does something for nothing. They are paid, not by you, but by the commissions charged in the products they sell you.

This can be excellent free advice or the most expensive you ever had. This depends on what happens to the product you buy. If you should lose all your invested capital, that's very costly advice. On the other hand, if you make a killing, your advisor may be the most wonderful person on earth!

Some No Fee Advisors, or financial planners, belong to the International Association of Financial Planners.

The IAFP maintains that a financial planner is a "generalist, knowledgeable in many fields," who "sets up tax strategy and an investment mix to get the maximum benefit" from the client's funds. Further, he must be a "highly professional counselor with a wide and thorough knowledge not only of investment opportunities but of the means of preserving, protecting and increasing the original investment." We have a difficult time believing that many people possess a "wide and thorough knowledge" of taxes, stocks, bonds, real estate, insurance, retirement plans, trust deeds, etc. We'd like to quote Dee Dee Ahern in a book we recommend, *The Economics of Being a Woman* (MacMillan, $8.95). "In our age of financial specialization, even the experts I interviewed knew little beyond their area of expertise."

You Can Be Your Own Best Advisor

As you can see, there are all sorts of people willing to give you advice. It's a growing area of business. Why? Because the laws and the economy are getting so complicated you need to be part accountant, lawyer, tax expert, investment advisor, insurance agent and seer to be an expert.

If you're confused, you're in good company. From top corporate executive to the newly-widowed woman wanting to invest insurance proceeds, we're all bewildered by today's economy. Our best advice to you is to surround yourself with professionals you can trust. And just as important, do not underestimate your own ability to learn.

You've made a start. You're reading this book. Next, why not look into some community resources? Adult education courses, workshops and seminars about money matters are often given at little or no cost. Even if the person giving the seminar is trying to sell you something, you can resist the temptation to buy and just soak in the knowledge.

The only research you need to do before attending one of these courses, workshops or seminars is to investigate the credentials of the teacher. If you can't do it beforehand, ask the teacher for a resume and the names of people who have attended previous classes. Usually a good reputation spreads fast. This advice applies to anyone to whom you go for advice.

Investment Letters

If you like getting mail and learning at home, there is a large quantity of investment letters to which you can subscribe. They vary from one-page mimeographed sheets put out by people who work on their kitchen tables to comprehensive statistical reports by firms like Moody's and Standard & Poor's.

Investment letters purport to offer information based on in-depth studies of various investment opportunities. Obviously, few people have the time or resources to do this themselves.

Remember, though, that these investment letters are aids, not answers. The company or person who publishes this information does it for profit. The research may or may not reflect your individual needs.

Precious Metals and Gems

Precious metals, and gems (particularly diamonds) have long

148

been a refuge for investors who lose confidence in their country's political and financial stability.

The most popular of the precious metals are platinum, gold and silver. Their prices seem to soar up when people question the validity of their country's paper currency. Then when confidence is restored, the speculative inflated value drops back to the real intrinsic value. You can make money in this roller coaster game and you can lose it. One thing is for sure—it's an investment full of action.

A recent article in a national periodical began with these words about diamonds. "There is nothing, absolutely nothing, commonplace about them." They weren't telling us women anything we didn't already know!

Until the 1970's, when Americans began losing confidence in the US dollar, diamonds were considered an adornment. The fact that diamonds held their value was a marvelous excuse for buying that piece of jewelry you were dying for anyway. But don't fool yourself! "Investment quality" diamonds are usually larger and of a finer quality than most of those mounted in jewelry. Approximately 1% of total diamond production meets the quality standards set for investment stones.

Alas, precious stones should never be worn. Normal elements in the air and contact against other objects as you move your hands normally will decrease their value. An investment stone should be kept in a sealed box together with a gemologist's certificate. Then lock the package in your safe deposit box.

Diamond dealers will tell you the price of these gems has been on a steady rise for the last forty years. That may make diamonds sound like a riskless investment. As you know, substantial rewards require substantial risks.

Some of the drawbacks are these. Diamonds are not liquid at all times. If you were forced to sell when demand was not high, you would take a loss.

There are "hidden" costs. Diamond dealers mark up their stones and make commissions just like other investment brokers. If you live in a small town, you may not have access to a qualified gem dealer. Your local jeweler rarely carries the quality of stones required for a good investment.

When you find a suitable stone, you should have sound independent appraisals made. In addition, you are responsible for the safekeeping of your gems and will probably want to have them insured. Appraisals and insurance cost money.

And, finally, while your money is invested in precious gems or metals, it is not earning interest.

Those are the drawbacks. On the other hand, if diamonds were to turn against a forty-year trend and drop in value, you could certainly enjoy wearing them. They'd look a lot prettier on your hand than some worthless stock or bond certificates!

Which One Is For You?

When was the last time you went to a smorgasbord? Or even a potluck supper? Part of the fun is that you find yourself sampling things you'd never try otherwise.

Filet mignon and baked potato eaters take a taste of chicken cacciatore or Swedish meatballs. Jello mold fanciers branch out to pickled herring. There's a real sense of adventure if you let it happen.

Sometimes you find out, to your surprise, that you've been missing a real treat. Or maybe all you find out is that you'll never try *that* again! But at least you tried.

Opening yourself up to new adventures involves some risk. Escargots, frog's legs, and shark are not for everyone. On the other hand, think what you may be missing if all you eat is "the same old thing"!

We've given you a real smorgasbord of investments. We hope you're excited about sampling a few of them. There you stand, mouth watering, asking yourself, "Where do I begin?"

Start with something that feels comfortable. Go with your feelings. Maybe you lingered a little longer over the tax shelter section than the others. Maybe when we asked you if you wanted to be a landlord, you were surprised to find yourself thinking, "Maybe!" Or possibly your eyes glittered as brightly as those diamonds when we talked about precious metals and gems.

Start, simply, with something that appeals to you. It doesn't have to be completely "rational." "I like diamonds, or apartment buildings, or tax shelters" is a good place to start investigating. Then take some time developing your interest. Use the help of as many experts as you can. Find the investment that works right for you and that makes sense for your unique economic situation and goals.

Remember those goals you listed at the beginning of this chapter? With confidence in yourself and the expert advice of professionals, when necessary, you can meet those goals by putting your money to work for you.

BOND RATINGS

Moody's	Standard & Poor's	Interpretation
Aaa	AAA	Highest Grade
Aa	AA	High Grade
A	A	Upper medium, medium, grade sound
Baa	BBB	Medium, good grade; some uncertainty
Ba	BB	Fair to good; lower medium; uncertainty
B	B	Fair; speculative features
Caa	CCC	Outright speculations; marked weakness
C	C	Best defaulted issues; highly speculative
Daa	DDD	In default
Da	DD	Assets of little value
D	D	No apparent Value

STATE	SECURITY DEVICES	MAXIMUM INTEREST RATES
Alabama	Mortgage	formula
Alaska	Deed of Trust	formula
Arizona	Deed of Trust	10%
Arkansas	Both	10%
California	Deed of Trust	10%
Colorado	Deed of Trust	formula
Connecticut	Mortgage	formula
Delaware	Mortgage	formula
Florida	Mortgage	10%
Georgia	Mortgage	9%
Hawaii	Mortgage	12%
Idaho	Deed of Trust	10%
Illinois	Deed of Trust	9½%
Indiana	Mortgage	8%
Iowa	Mortgage	9%
Kansas	Mortgage	10%
Kentucky	Both	8½%
Maine	Both	formula
Maryland	Both	12%
Massachusetts	Mortgage	18%
Michigan	Mortgage	7%
Minnesota	Mortgage	8%
Mississippi	Deed of Trust	10%
Missouri	Deed of Trust	10%
Montana	Deed of Trust	10%
Nebraska	Deed of Trust	11%
Nevada	Deed of Trust	12%
New Hampshire	Mortgage	any rate
New Jersey	Mortgage	9½%
New Mexico	Deed of Trust	10%
New York	Mortgage	8½%
North Carolina	Deed of Trust	12%
North Dakota	Mortgage	9%
Ohio	Mortgage	8%
Oklahoma	Mortgage	10%
Oregon	Deed of Trust	10%
Pennsylvania	Mortgage	8%
Rhode Island	Mortgage	15%

STATE	SECURITY DEVICES	MAXIMUM INTEREST RATES
South Carolina	Mortgage	9%
South Dakota	Mortgage	10%
Tennessee	Deed of Trust	10%
Texas	Deed of Trust	10%
Utah	Deed of Trust	formula
Vermont	Mortgage	formula
Virginia	Deed of Trust	12%
Washington	Deed of Trust	12%
West Virginia	Deed of Trust	8%
Wisconsin	Mortgage	formula
Wyoming	Mortgage	formula

Where credit is due

Credit is an aspect of our economy which has grown and changed until today, we have not just a nation, but a world, where you can pull out a little plastic card and say, "Charge it." Early prejudices against overspending and being "up to the ears" in debt is changing. Now we have a much more accepting attitude toward the credit concept. In this chapter, we will not deal with the question of whether you are able to resist over-buying when you have a credit card. We will focus, instead, on your rights to equal credit opportunities.

Until very recent legislation, women as a group have been discriminated against when it came to granting credit. The creditor was free to indulge in personal assumptions about the status and behavior of women. Creditors generally had negative sterotypes about women's willingness and ability to pay and very often credit was refused. Single women were given less favorable terms and limits than men in the same financial bracket. Ordinarily happy housewives found themselves chagrined and looking into "Women's Lib" when the credit card they had applied for came back with their husband's name on it.

Aggravation over the name appearing on the card turned into frustration when the wife found herself widowed or divorced with no credit in her own name. Somehow, all those payments she sent in so conscientiously, and perhaps out of her own earnings, only enhanced her *husband's* standing with the credit information bureaus.

155

have changed. It is illegal to discriminate but it
you to assert your right to a good credit reputa-
ou never really expect to need it. There are new
laws to help single and married women obtain credit but it is
up to each woman to take advantage of the laws and plan
ahead.

It is certainly better to have an excellent credit rating and
never use it than it is to really need some credit and not be in
a position to obtain it. It is certainly better to *know* that you
have established a credit reputation than discover too late
that you have no credit in your own name. Remember, there
are certain big purchases such as a home and car which just
about everybody buys on credit rather than outright. What
follows are some hints on what to do if you want a sterling
name in the credit realm.

Obviously, it is up to you once you have acquired such a
reputation to keep it untarnished. Credit only postpones and
spreads out expenses. It does not eliminate them! Credit can
also be expensive in terms of interest rates. The percentage
you pay is clearly set out on the contract and it is up to you to
decide whether it is worth it for you.

Putting Your Best Foot Forward In the Credit Office

Basically, credit is any transaction where you receive goods
and services with the seller trusting you to pay later. If someone were to approach you and ask you to lend them some
money, you would quickly go through a personal evaluation
process on whether they were a "good risk." This process
might be nothing more than an unconscious checklist that
you never really considered before. Similarly, the large institutions have their own "checklists" which have become very
standardized with the passage of time, and now, due to
nondiscrimination laws, must be more concise than ever.

The places where you seek credit do not *have* to extend
credit to you. They only have to apply the same checklist to
you that they apply to other people. The credit application
will most likely contain many and varied questions. You may

consider it annoyingly personal, but you are asking a favor of them and they, in turn, want to be sure they will not be left "holding the bag."

We are not defending the questions that are asked. It isn't too hard to come up with a variety of examples where conscientious people are denied credit while outright crooks may obtain it. What we will share with you is what sort of a profile is the most appealing one in the creditor's eye.

The most obvious source of money that you will use to repay debts is a steady paycheck or other form of consistent income. Another thing that the creditor is going to consider is your past credit history. You will find yourself being asked about credit cards you may already have as well as checking and savings accounts in your own name. Other things looked for are prompt payments in the past, home ownership or long-term rental, and no defaults on loans.

A creditor will also look at current indebtedness. As a matter of fact, there is even a system to find out whether you are "up to your ears" in debts. Potential creditors calculate your "debt ratio." Your debt ratio is a comparison between your after-tax income and what you owe (except for home mortgage or rental payments). If you have an after-tax income of $10,000 and owed $2,000, this would be a twenty percent ratio which is considered good. If you want to look at this optimistically, you might consider that while the creditor protecting himself from the deadbeats she is also preventing you from getting in an uncomfortable position of being overwhelmed by bills you can't afford to pay.

What the Creditor Will View as a Poor Risk

Remember that these are the guidelines which the creditor has established over a period of time to protect his company. You may be a person who conscientiously and cheerfully pays every debt off before it is due and yet fall into the "poor risk" category as far as creditors are concerned. We did not make the rules but we want you to be aware of them before you set foot in the credit office.

The opposite of what we have described as a "good risk" will be considered a "poor risk." Frequent job changes, no or unsteady employment, inconsistent income, slow payment of debts, no bank accounts, no credit in your own name and a transient living situation always look bad on applications. You may have a very interesting story to explain all of this but you had best take it to a publisher, not a potential creditor.

What's in a Name?

At least as old as the tradition of extending credit has been the tradition of a married woman's taking on the last name of her husband. The widow or the divorcee may suddenly discover for the first time that she has been relying solely on her husband's credit cards and credit reputation. As is often the case, even the telephone and utilities are or were in his name. The best time to establish credit is before the death or divorce of a spouse. Hopefully, we have reached you in time. Even if you are reading this with a feeling of regret since you are already experiencing the credit difficulties of the widowed or divorced woman, at least you are wiser now. At some future date, there may be another marriage and you will certainly approach this credit issue differently.

You Have Rights—Both State and Federal

It is important for you to understand your rights under the laws that insure equal credit opportunity for women. The Federal Equal Credit Opportunity Act (The Act), effective October, 1975 prohibits discrimination against any applicant for consumer credit on the basis of sex, marital status, race, religion, national origin, age or receipt of public assistance benefits. Besides the issues of sex and marital status, it may be important for you to keep in mind the other prohibitions, especially with regard to age and public assistance.

The Act applies to all creditors who extend credit in the regular course of their business, such as banks, stores, restaurants—even doctors and dentists. The law covers you the moment you contact the creditor. This means that even something which is *said* to you to discourage you from applying for credit on the grounds of sex, marital status or any of the previously mentioned grounds, is in violation of the law. Of course, it is difficult to prove what was *said* on the telephone or in person but it doesn't hurt to be aware of your rights. The best evidence of discrimination is the denial of a completed application for credit submitted by an otherwise qualified person. In addition to the federal law, many *states* have laws to further protect your rights. They cannot diminish what the federal government has already legislated. Of course, the creditor has to comply with all laws, both state and federal.

Separate and Equal

In the past, creditors denied the right of a married woman to establish a separate account in her own name. Discrimination on the basis of one's marital status is now prohibited. The big exception is in connection with applications for secured credit. There is one partial exception. In a community property state, the creditor may ask if the person is married, unmarried or separated (but not whether she is divorced or widowed).

Often women get hung up on what name they should use. Actually, a woman may apply for credit in her maiden name, married name, or a combination of both. Courtesy titles such as Ms., Miss or Mrs. are optional and the applicant has the right to refuse to supply that information.

Community Spirit

If you live in one of ten community property states, the federal law makes special reference to your particular situation. We will use California as an example but since there are differences in the laws of the various community property states you may need to do some further investigation. In California,

a wife or husband can list all community property in applying for credit, including spouse's salary. Thus, it would be entirely legal for a wife to approach the same company where
her husband already had individual credit and apply for her
own account, listing all the same assets which her husband
already used.

Questions That Must Remain Unasked

Creditors are no longer allowed to ask anything and everything in a sort of "fact finding" expedition into your personal
financial world. You may be happy to know that some very
personal questions are no longer legal. If you are a woman in
your childbearing years, it would be tempting for a creditor
to ask about birth control or childbearing capability, but is
illegal since it would not be asked of men. If you are getting
spousal or child support, that is an obvious clue that you are
divorced. You do not have to disclose these sources of income
unless you are relying on them as a basis for credit.

Answering questions about your spouse is a pretty obvious
clue to your marital status. There are, however, three instances where you would be required to give information
about your spouse: (1) if the spouse signs the credit application or will use the account; (2) if the applicant is relying on
income from the spouse; and (3) if community property is a
basis for credit.

A negative credit rating cannot be assigned solely on the
basis of age. If the applicant is considered "elderly,"
creditors may consider how an upcoming retirement may affect income. If you feel that your age has been a factor in
refusal for credit, don't sit back and accept it. You need to let
creditors know that *you* know your rights. In the process, you
will not only help yourself but others who come after you.

Co-signatures: When There Are Two Dotted Lines

Incredible stories of chagrin and embarrassment have been
passed on to us concerning co-signatures. Women of all ages

and economic circumstances have been told they must find a "reliable male" to co-sign the loan or credit application. Women, working and earning very adequate salaries, often had to ask their fathers, husbands, even grandfathers or brothers, to co-sign loans.

Thank goodness all that has changed! The law now prohibits a creditor from requiring a co-signer unless such a requirement is imposed on all similarly qualified applicants who apply for the same type and amount of credit. Creditors cannot legally require co-signatures for all married applicants because that would be discrimination on the basis of marital status. They, of course, cannot require co-signatures all women because that would be sex discrimination.

Now that we have made a blanket assertion, we will back up and cover the very exceptions to the rule and explain how they apply. If a lien or transfer to the title of property is required, as it would be in a secured credit transaction, the non-applicant spouse may be required to sign the documents necessary to create the lien or transfer.

Community property states again pop up their unique heads. If you live in a community property state and you do not have "management and control" over sufficient community property or sufficient separate property to qualify for credit, your spouse's signature may be required. The degrees of management and control vary in each of the community property states. In California, for example, the wife has full management and control which means that the co-signature will generally not be required.

One final credit application to consider is the "joint account." Naturally, when a husband and wife apply for a joint account, both sign and both are personally liable on the account.

What Is Fair to Consider?

We have been going on and on about getting credit without talking about how *much* credit you might expect to get. This

Alone

matter may get a little touchy with some divorced women because while the creditor may not discount an applicant's income from spousal and child support, he may ask questions about the former spouse if this category of income is listed for consideration. The creditor wants to know whether the husband is likely to continue these payments. Thus he can ask questions about the former spouse just as he can about the applicant. Standard questions asked are the length of time over which payments have been made, the regularity of their receipt and whether the payments are made pursuant to a written agreement or court decree. As if these additional questions didn't complicate things enough, the Fair Credit Reporting Act limits the information which may be made available about a former spouse. Without the ex-spouse's written consent, consumer reporting agencies may not release information to creditors for transactions not involving the spouse.

If you are contemplating divorce, this last point is important to consider. Women who are currently negotiating divorce settlement agreements should talk to their attorneys about credit provisions. The husband should agree to provide appropriate written approval for the release of credit information.

Besides spousal and child support, a woman may also list part-time employment, public assistance benefits, pensions and social security. The part-time aspect is of special interest to women. Previously, when it was often not included, this discriminated much more against women than men (women make up the majority of the part-time work force). While creditors can no longer automatically exclude the part-time income, they may consider whether it comes from seasonal work or they may consider how long the applicant has been employed at the part-time job.

It may appear as if we have been answering the riddle "When is discrimination not discrimination?" Nobody is interested in giving credit if you aren't going to pay it back. All these new laws have been done to insure that you, as a woman, will not be excluded specifically because you are a woman.

Sometimes, social mores and problems make even apparently fair policies discriminatory. Let's take for example the listing of a phone in one's own name. Creditors used to assign "points" or other positive scoring devices for a phone listing in an applicant's name. Yet, fear of obscene phone calls or worse prevents a vast number of women from listing phones in their own names. Conventionally, married women have always had the listing in their husband's name. Here is a case where women used to lose out almost unanimously. Now, a creditor may choose to assign a value to *having* a telephone, no matter whose name it's under.

Making History

Most of us are vaguely aware that somewhere in the world there are big computers in credit reporting agencies which keep track of how reliable we are in our use of credit. In a way, our transactions have been writing history. We soon found out that we needed a good credit history in order to obtain more credit. Traditionally, accounts held or used jointly by spouses were submitted to credit reporting agencies using only the *husband's* name. A divorced or widowed woman soon discovered, to her dismay, that all the good history she thought she was making by conscientiously paying the bills was actually being written only under her husband's name.

Finally, things are changing. On accounts established on or after June 1, 1977, the law requires that creditors maintain the account and submit credit information in the name of both spouses if the account is jointly held or used. On accounts established prior to that date, the creditor may do one of two things. She may automatically maintain and report the account in the name of both spouses. Or, she may simply advise married couples in writing that they have the right to request and have all accounts maintained under both names.

All of this has been focused on the "light" side of credit

where everything is going well. What about the situation where your spouse has been a bad example as a credit user? He has been unreliable and you fear your good name in the credit history book is ruined. Just as the new law provides for a woman who may wish to use the good payment record of a spouse or ex-spouse to establish a good credit history, the law provides a way for a woman to disassociate herself from the "bad" credit history of her spouse or ex-spouse. This is particularly helpful when the woman has been required to sign business loans and hasn't had control over the repayment. In either case, a woman attempting to get credit can come forward with evidence showing it was really *she* who signed the checks and saw that the payments were made *or* , if the payments were not made, that it was her *husband*, not herself, who was at fault. The creditor *must consider* the information given by the applicant in making a determination of credit worthiness.

The Name Change Game

Many years ago, a woman by the name of Lucy Stone defied the conventions of American etiquette by keeping her own name after her marriage. The trend hasn't caught on yet but the credit practices that made this a wise move have now been ameliorated. In the past, it was standard practice for creditors to close the accounts of women who underwent a change of name or marital status. It didn't matter to the creditor whether this was due to marriage, divorce or widowhood. Now, if the account holder is "contractually liable" on an account—you signed it yourself—the creditor cannot terminate or alter the account merely because of a change of name or marital status.

Once again we must get back to credit as a loan on the expectation that the money can and will be repaid. If there is some evidence that the account holder has become unable or unwilling to pay, the creditor may take action. If the applicant's spouse was the sole source of income, or if the woman was merely a user and not really the applicant on the account, the creditor may require re-application.

New laws also require that you know within a reasonable period of time, and if your application for credit was refused ("adverse action") the reason why. There are other things besides outright refusal which are also considered adverse action. Such things as refusal to increase credit limit, termination and unfavorable changes in terms not affecting substantially all other similar accounts. You are entitled to hear adverse action and the reason why within thirty days.

Summary

You may or may not be a good credit risk. What we have tried to share with you in this chapter is *how* a creditor may go about attempting to decide whether or not to extend credit to you. Most emphatically, we have been saying, creditors may no longer discriminate against you on a basis of sex or marital status. If you need help on your particular credit problems, or feel you have been discriminated against, you should investigate the sources of help in your area. Women's groups such as NOW often provide the names of attorneys or public service organizations who are experienced in all aspects of women's rights. Many local law schools or universities have a women's center which may provide counselors knowledgeable about federal and state credit laws. In addition, the following government agencies may be contacted about certain types of credit discrimination.

1. Credit discrimination by retail stores, credit card issuers and finance companies:
    Federal Trade Commission
    Washington, D.C.
    (or local office)
2. Credit discrimination by national banks:
    Comptroller of Currency
    Washington, D.C.
3. Credit discrimination by state banks:
    Federal reserve bank serving your area
4. The local District Attorney's Office

When to take coverage

If you are a worrier, this is the chapter where you can really indulge in some nightmarish "catastrophic expectations." What if you were severely injured in a car accident? Could you afford to pay the medical bills? What if you were disabled and permanently without income? What if a fire destroyed your house and all your personal possessions? What if you accidentally injured someone? Could you afford a liability suit for $100,000? These are not pleasant things to consider. But they can and do happen every day. They can happen to you. No matter how much money you manage to have in your savings and investments, chances are you would never be able to handle the "worst" if any of these things should actually happen to you.

Insurance is your protection against what might happen but you hope will not. The insurance company bets that it will not happen to you. If you choose to buy insurance, then you are protecting yourself against the possibility that it will. We will guide you through the mystifying terminology and reality of the wide world of insurance.

There are all kinds of insurance to cover all kinds of situations. Film stars, for example, have been known to insure the parts of their anatomies that have made them famous. Thus, certain faces, legs, and even busts have been insured. Policies like these are shortlived. In fact, they are usually obtained only for their publicity value. They do, however, demonstrate that you can insure just about *anything*.

167

For the majority of us, homeowner's, renter's, life, health, burial, disability and fire insurance are the ones that will meet our needs. Chances are you will not even need all of these. We will explore all of them so that you will know what is available. You can then assess your own needs and decide what insurance to buy.

Policy Roundup

There are many different types of insurance coverage. As a married couple, you and your husband probably had your car, home and personal belongings insured. You also probably had medical and life insurance.

If you are facing divorce or probate, one of your organizational goals will be to determine what insurance you presently carry. You need to review your coverage for legal proceedings. You will also want to take this opportunity to educate yourself. As a single woman, you want to intelligently reevaluate and provide for your unique insurance needs.

How do you determine what insurance you actually have? Often, this is not as easy as it sounds. Ideally, you have an insurance file. This is one fireproof location for all the policies you possess. Since most people are well-intentioned but disorganized, we suggest you conduct your search with these additional steps:

1. Review the contents of your safe deposit box at the bank.

2. Check your "important paper" files for summaries or references to policies.

3. Review your checkbook for premium payments over the last several years.

4. Check with the agents or brokers that have handled your insurance in the past.

5. Write to any insurance company with which you think you might have a policy.

6. If you know you have coverage and have lost the policy, request that a duplicate policy be issued.

After you've accumulated all the insurance policies you

can find, carefully review them for dates, content and coverage. It is not unusual to have old, "lapsed" policies lying around. Check dates to see which ones have expired. Check to make sure they have been renewed or replaced.

Make sure your insurance policies are kept in a fireproof container *in your home.* Since they are non-negotiable, they are of no interest to burglars and do not need to be put in your safe deposit box. It is very inconvenient to have them in safe deposit boxes. Instead, put a *list* of the policies by company name and policy number in your safe deposit box, with a notation giving the location of the policy. Include the agent's name and phone number. That way, if a policy is lost or destroyed, it will be easy for you to replace it by referring to the list in your safe deposit box and then calling your agent or broker.

What To Ask

You will also want to review the protection afforded by each policy. We will list the most common types of insurance with a brief description of the coverage under each. You can fill in the details by reading your own policy. This, however, can be an extremely "strange encounter." (To the average person, insurance policy writers seem to be visitors from another planet!)

It is more realistic simply to review the cover page of your policy, which lists amounts and dates of coverage, premium amounts and other details. Then, with your policy in hand, call or visit your insurance broker or agent and ask her to give you a written explanation in "plain English" of what it's all about. Turn this into a real learning experience. Ask her whether you have "minimum" or other coverage. Ask her why she recommended this particular coverage and if she sees any need for change considering your new circumstances. Ask her specifically if she thinks you have adequate protection and also if there is any cheaper way to obtain the same coverage. Insist that she give you an explanation of the policy and the answers to your questions in writing, and in language you can understand.

The reason you will want your insurance agent's answers in writing is so you can take them to your attorney and financial advisor. You need their opinions, too! If you try to relay information verbally from agent to attorney or agent to financial advisor, it can get to be like that "telephone" game we played as children. You know, the game where you whisper the "message" quickly around the circle and it's hysterically garbled by the time it gets back to the originator. That was fun at a birthday party but it's extremely frustrating and inefficient in real life. Get it in writing!

Insurance for All Seasons (And Circumstances)

Automobile insurance provides you with liability, medical payments, comprehensive (including fire and theft) and collision coverage. Liability coverage may be required by law in the state where you live. This protects you against liability arising from any injury or damage you may cause as a driver. We recommend that you have at least $300,000 automobile liability coverage (unless your state requires more, of course).

Automobile insurance can give you a variety of coverages. We will describe the six most basic of these with which you should be familiar.

Bodily injury liability—This covers death or bodily injury to victims of an accident caused by you or a person driving your car with your permission.

Collision—No matter who is to blame for a collision with a car or object, this insurance covers damage to your car. There may be a $50 to $200 deductible.

Comprehensive—This protects your car in the event of vandalism, theft, flood, fire, lightning, explosions, falling objects, collision with an animal and more.

Uninsured motorist—Not all motorists have insurance. If one

170

of these uninsured motorists hits you and it's his fault, you're insured by your company.

Property damage liability—If your car does damage to someone else's property, this insurance pays for the damage.

Medical—No matter who is at fault in an accident, this policy covers medical expenses for you and any passengers in your car. It also covers you as a passenger in another car.

Homeowner's insurance. If you own your home, you should arrange for a homeowner's "package policy" which includes fire and casualty coverage.

The fire insurance coverage under your homeowner's package policy should provide coverage for at least eighty percent of the replacement value of your house. Replacement value does not mean the price you paid for your house. It means how much it would cost you to replace your house, new, today. Building costs are rising yearly. This means your coverage must increase proportionately.

If your house is mortgaged, you are probably required by your lender to carry a specified minimum amount of fire insurance naming the lender as the loss payee. This way the lender is assured of being paid back the amount of money he lent you for your house if it burns down. (After all, your house was the security for the loan.) The lender is automatically notified of any changes in coverage or cancellation of your insurance coverage for nonpayment of premiums.

If you do not own your own home or live in an apartment or condominium, you can arrange for a similar *tenant's* homeowner's policy.

Fire and theft insurance may be included in your homeowner's policy to cover personal property such as furniture and clothing. You can get coverage based on the replacement cost of these items or on an actual cash value basis (what the destroyed items are worth today, considering how old they are, normal wear and tear, etc.).

If a fire were to destroy all the contents of your home, today, you'd probably have trouble coming up with a list of everything you had lost. For this reason, insurance companies suggest that you photograph each room in your house. Instead, you might prefer to make a very detailed written inventory of every item in every room. You should store the photographs or list in your safe deposit box at the bank. (Note the location of the inventory or photographs in your metal file.)

In addition to fire, a homeowner's policy covers you for personal liability. This kind of insurance protects you from liability if someone is injured in an accident other than one involving an automobile or business. For example, suppose a guest trips over a roller skate on your front porch and hurts herself? Suppose your dog bites a visiting child? We recommend that you have at least $300,000 personal liability coverage.

Umbrella liability coverage protects you against large liability claims which might be financially devastating. We recommend you consider umbrella coverage of at least $1,000,000. However, you should discuss this with your personal insurance professional. Umbrella coverage provides coverage above the $300,000 we have recommended for both automobile and personal liability limits.

Personal article floaters are available for special personal property. Under a normal homeowner's policy, items such as furs and jewelry are only insured to a total of $500. If you have some very valuable personal possessions, any anticipated loss in excess of this $500 should be specifically scheduled under a personal articles floater.

Theft insurance, which is normally included in your homeowner's policy, covers the unlawful taking of your property. It is the broad term for loss by:

1. Burglary or forcible entry into premises for the purpose of stealing; and

2. Robbery or the taking of property from a person by force or threat of force.

Health insurance. This type of policy reimburses you for medical expenses which you and your family incur. Health insurance coverage usually includes hospitalization, laboratory bills, doctor bills and medication. Reimbursement is rarely for the full amount of the expense. A typical schedule would be reimbursement for 80% of all expenses after a $50, $100 or $200 deductible has been met either by you individually or by your family as a whole. Such policies are issued to a group of employees (Group Insurance) or to just you and your family (Individual Insurance). Premiums for group insurance are usually much cheaper. Check to see if you have an option to convert your coverage from your husband's group plan to an individual plan if you suddenly find you will not have any health insurance coverage in your new status. This is usually cheaper than obtaining your own individual coverage. You will also want to convert coverage for your children if possible. (In the case of divorce, be sure to have your attorney negotiate dependent coverage for the children in your divorce settlement.)

We have a word of caution for you. Never buy health (or casualty) insurance from ads in the Sunday newspaper. Advertisements can be very misleading. Endorsements by television celebrities do not guarantee quality in insurance coverage. The policy may sound great but check the fine print. It may turn out you're only covered if you are trampled by a herd of elephants while attending a bullfight in Tijuana, Mexico, on the third Sunday of a month which has thirty days. Recently, due to some conscientious insurance commissioners, the Sunday supplement insurance advertising has been getting more ethical. Still, you must not rely on Madison Avenue techniques to make a wise insurance decision.

Disability income insurance replaces your earned income if you become disabled and unable to earn money. You may also be eligible for social security and state disability coverage if you are disabled. In addition to this you may also purchase an individual policy that will pay you a stated amount after you have been disabled for a certain period (elimination period).

Life insurance is the type of policy which pays a death benefit to the named beneficiary of the policy at the death of the person insured (as long as the premiums have been paid). Basically life insurance policies fall into three major categories: term insurance, whole life (ordinary or straight) insurance, and savings type life insurance.

1. *Term insurance*—As the name implies, this type of insurance lasts only for the term of the policy. For example, one year, five years, ten years, or until you reach age sixty-five. It is somewhat like renting or leasing the coverage. These policies are generally renewable and named "renewable term." This means you can renew the coverage at the end of the term without proof of insurability, up to the age sixty-five or seventy. This could be valuable if you knew you had a terminal illness. The policies are generally convertible to other forms of life insurance policies with level premiums. This means that instead of having your premium go up each time you renewed, you could change to a policy which would keep the same premium. Or you could also convert to a policy with death benefits that last beyond age sixty-five or so. Term insurance premiums *increase* with age and your policy does not accumulate any cash value. Mortgage insurance is nothing more than term insurance that pays off a mortgage when the insured dies. Because it is called mortgage insurance you may pay more for it. It may or may not be required by your lender, but you can anticipate being barraged by sales pitches on why you should buy it.

2. *Whole life insurance*—This insurance stays in force until you discontinue paying premiums or until the death of the insured. The premium is established at the time you purchase the policy and remains level through the life of the policy. These policies are easily identified because they generate a cash value based upon the time period that you have held the policy. (In this sense, the policy's cash value is considered an asset.) You can borrow against the cash value or terminate

your policy and receive a check for the cash value at that time.

Because whole life insurance gives you not only insurance on your life but a forced savings plan, the premium is higher. Depending upon your ability to save money and your sophistication in the world of finance, the forced savings aspect of this kind of policy can be an advantage or a disadvantage. If you have no self-discipline when it comes to saving money, a whole life policy will guarantee this discipline. On the other hand, with sound financial advice, you can make a better investment than handing it over to your insurance company which does not allow you to participate in the profits of all those big buildings they own.

3. *Savings type life insurance*—These policies are designed primarily to provide a savings vehicle with a self-completing arrangement. This means if you die before the target date for your savings plan, the rest of the money will be provided by the insurance policy. These policies are called retirement income or endowment policies. Annuities are total savings type plans.

An *endowment policy* is a policy in which you pay premiums for a designated time period. At maturity the policy holder receives the face value if she is living. If she dies before maturity the insurance proceeds go to her beneficiary.

An *annuity* is a contract with an insurance company. You give the company a sum of money. In turn, the insurance company guarantees to pay you a stated income for a stated period of time or, more commonly, for as long as you live.

In an inflationary economy you'll need more than an insurance contract to get you through your retirement years.

Once you have rounded up any insurance policies you can find, you will want to evaluate your coverage. We recommend the help of an insurance professional. These people are very knowledgeable in their field but always remember, they make their living selling insurance.

Choosing an Insurance Professional

Property and casualty insurance is available from many insurance agents and brokers. An insurance *agent* is appointed directly by an insurance company to act as its agent. She works for only one company. On the other hand, an *independent agent* is the appointed representative of more than one insurance company. An insurance *broker* represents the insured (you) and not an insurance company.

If you have already selected an insurance agent or broker, and you feel comfortable with her advice and judgment, it is probably fine to stay with her. Remember, though, an insurance professional is just that. Her expertise is limited to the field of insurance. Any advice she may offer on such matters as ownership of property, wills and trusts, etc., should be weighed with the advice of your attorney and financial advisor.

If you feel a change is in order, we recommend that you consider an independent agent who represents several different companies. Independent agents can "shop" the insurance markets for you, and hopefully obtain the broadest protection at the lowest price.

Service is important in all property and casualty insurance. In the event you have to file a claim, you will want a convenient, local agent. It's also helpful to ask your friends. Was their experience with the agent who handled their claims worse than the event that necessitated it? Who do they recommend?

The old adage, "You get what you pay for" is certainly true in insurance. If you seem to have a terrific deal on the amount of premium you pay for your health, automobile or disability insurance, you had better check the fine print. A low premium may indicate a very high deductible or less than adequate coverage. Conversely, a high premium may be the result of an unnecessarily low deductible. For example, if you have a fine driving record you will probably want to go with a fairly high deductible in order to save on your insurance premiums. On the other hand, if you have a history of "fender benders" a low deductible will offer you some financial assistance through your insurance company. This, however, would eventually affect your premiums. The important thing is to be aware of the various advantages and disadvantages and discuss them with your broker in order to get the most for your money.

In the area of insurance, as in many other business fields, there are professionals. Property and casualty insurance agents who meet certain professional qualifications are entitled to use the initials CPCU after their names (similar to a CPA for accountants). CPCU stands for Chartered Property and Casualty Underwriter. Likewise, you will want to look for a CLU in life insurance (Chartered Life Underwriter). This gives you assurance that they are experienced and subscribe to an insurance code of ethics.

Making Changes in Your Coverage

The owner of a policy has the right to make changes in coverage, change beneficiaries or borrow from any cash value available in any policy. Since the owner, the beneficiary and the insured can be three different people, the attorney settling your divorce or closing probate can establish the owner of your policies for you. You may contact your agent or broker or your employer, in the case of Group Insurance, for forms to make any changes that you desire. You can deal directly with the insurance company, but it is usually more efficient to use an agent or broker. Normally, you should plan to make changes in policies with expiration dates at the time just before expiration to avoid a "short rate" cancellation penalty.

Getting Your Claims Paid

If one of those "catastophic expectations" comes true, you will need to process a claim for liability, fire, casualty or theft. The simplest approach is to contact the agent or broker who sold you the insurance. She will probably have a claims adjuster contact you. You then tell the details of the loss to the adjuster. You'll be asked to provide whatever proof of loss is required.

Health insurance, long term disability or death claims are processed on insurance company forms obtained from your agent or broker. It saves time to send the completed forms directly to the insurance company. Contact your agent or broker only if you have questions on the data needed or if you feel the claim has not been paid properly.

Hopefully, all will proceed swiftly and smoothly. If you are disappointed and feel that your claim has not been paid properly and your agent or broker has not been able to persuade the insurance company to change its mind, you do have recourse. You can file a complaint with the Insurance Commissioner of the state where you live. Insurance Commissioners are very responsive to consumer complaints. Usually just the threat of contacting the Insurance Commissioner is a very persuasive pressure on an insurance company. If all this fails, you can discuss with your attorney the possibility of filing suit against the carrier. Certainly this is grief added to grief but it *is* an option.

Your Unique Insurance Needs

As a single woman, responsible for your own financial security, insurance is just as important to you as planned savings and investing. When you begin to adjust to your single status, you will want to make informed decisions about insurance to protect yourself and your dependents from financial disaster.

Liability, fire, theft, health insurance and long-term disability coverage *must be valued against* your potential risks, premium charged, and the result to your overall financial condition if you had to pay for any losses out of your assets.

Life insurance must first be valued upon other people's dependence on you. If you happen to be one of those unusual women with no one dependent upon you then you may not need life insurance. However, many people with no one dependent on them like to have several thousand dollars of insurance for their funeral and burial so they are not a burden after their death. On the other hand, your children may be dependent upon your income to raise and educate them, or there may be a disabled child's needs for the future, the needs of dependent parents—retired, disabled or financially insecure. Secondly, life insurance must be valued upon your desire to pass your estate to your heirs. Insurance can provide the cash to pay estate taxes so the estate can be passed intact to your heirs without being reduced or partially sold off. (Life insurance, properly arranged, can be kept out of the estate of the insured.)

A final word of caution: sometimes life insurance is "sold," not "bought." As we mentioned you may not need any at all! If so don't let anyone sell it to you. What types of insurance you need, and how much, are personal decisions. Our best advice is that you select a Chartered Property and Casualty Underwriter (CPCU) or Chartered Life Underwriter (CLU) in your own community who has a reputation for providing good service. Ask him to tailor an insurance program to fit your specific needs. Before committing yourself, weigh his advice with that of your attorney and financial advisor.

You can't take it with you
but your heirs may think you did

This chapter is probably the most unpleasant because it deals with two most unsavory topics for human beings. Those two topics are: death and taxes. Another topic which is touched upon, which is equally unpleasant, but not thought about as often, is legal fees.

Many women, when they hear the word *estate* picture a large white mansion with a circular driveway and a rolling green expanse of lawn. Since they do not have one of these, they feel they do not need to do any estate planning. Actually, an estate is everything that you have accumulated during your lifetime. There are very few of us who have not accumulated something along the way. This is why estate planning is so important. If what we gathered was important enough for us to work for and take into our own name, it is equally important that we have some assurance who will receive these things when we can no longer use them.

What is estate planning? A fancy, technical definition might read, "Estate planning is the creation, preservation and devolution of an individual's accumulated wealth to her intended beneficiaries." However, looking beyond this fancy language, what we really see is the creation of wealth, preservation of wealth and the transference of wealth, either during one's lifetime or at death, to the people that we wish to enjoy it after we are through enjoying it.

181

We have talked about the creation and preservation of what will be considered your estate in our chapters in budgeting and investing. Here we will talk about the devolution of your estate. We are working on the assumption that, while you may not have a stately, white mansion with manicured lawns and gardens, you do have possessions which you will increase or at least maintain until the time you die. Most people are quite surprised when they start thinking about their cars, the equity they have built up in their homes, other property that they possess, stocks, bonds, savings and insurance, about how large an estate they actually do have. People are equally surprised at the tremendous bites that taxes and legal fees may take out of an estate before it passes on to loved ones. Likewise, we have all seen traumatic situations where the estate did not get distributed in the way we believed the decedent wished. Contemplating your own death is not the most pleasant thing to think about. After contemplating what may happen to your possessions upon your demise, you will want to do appropriate estate planning.

The devolution of your estate is the transference of wealth, either during your lifetime or at your death, to those whom you have intended to be your beneficiaries. There are always those people who might be parasites and lie or misrepresent that you really intended them to be your beneficiaries. This is what you want to avoid. Therefore, we are concerned here with protecting your assets and guaranteeing that your assets do, in fact, efficiently become the assets of those loved ones whom you desire to benefit by your estate in this transfer.

Can you afford to die? Let's discuss high costs of dying and how to avoid them. First, we must consider what the high costs of dying are. Most of us are aware that when we pass away we will probably have last illness expenses, funeral expenses, and debts. However, these are not the high costs of dying which we are referring to. The high costs of dying which, typically, greatly reduce one's estate so that beneficiaries do not, in fact, truly realize the full value of what we own at our death are: death taxes and probate.

There are basically two types of death taxes, the Federal

Estate Tax, and the State Inheritance Tax. These death taxes are, in fact, *transfer* taxes. They are taxes on the assets of the individual who passes away. Really, they are taxes on her right to transfer assets to her intended beneficiaries. If you died with $100,000, and then transfer that $100,000 to Jane Doe, you have transferred $100,000 of wealth. The federal and state governments tax a percentage of that $100,000 when it is transferred to Jane Doe.

Many persons confuse death taxes with probate. Probate is a legislatively enacted system to guarantee that the decedent's intent is, in fact, carried out. What this means is that the court becomes involved to make sure that beneficiaries do, in fact, receive that which the decedent intended them to receive; that creditors are notified and paid; and that sufficient accounting controls and standards are met to protect the intentions of the decedent.

So far this may sound all well and good. However, there are a number of factors about probate which make it a most unpleasant process. Probate in many instances may take as long as two years to complete or even longer. It is also expensive. In most states, attorney's and executor's fees are not based on the amount of work or time put into performing the probate process. Rather, fees are set on a percentage of the assets passing through the probate. In addition to the attorney's fees, executor's fees, and administration expenses, there is also the inconvenience of having to endure as much as a year or two of "red tape" as all the assets are subjected to the court system of the county and state where the decedent lived. As if this were not enough, if an individual owned real property in states other than that within which she dies leaving only a simple will, then there are ancillary probate administration processes in every state where the decedent owned real property. Finally, what goes on in a probate process is public knowledge or a matter of public record, thereby exposing the heirs to possible exploitation by con artists. All in all, time-wise, expense-wise, and privacy-wise, the probate process is not an appealing one.

Fortunately, there are ways to avoid probate and some

death taxes. It is generally to our benefit to avoid death taxes and probate fees wherever possible. We should pay only that which we feel is warranted and avoid inconvenience and red tape whenever possible. Therefore, it comes down to the fact that every reader of this book will have to consider how her assets will be transferred at death. Basically, there are six methods. All of them have different tax and probate consequences. Here is a list of the six basic ways. Each of us will have our estate handled in one of these ways upon our death. Number one is what happens when we do nothing. Number two is what happens when we have a simple will. Number three is what happens when we have a Totten Trust. Number four is what happens if everything we own is in joint tenancy. Number five is what happens if we have set up a testamentary trust. Number six is what will happen if we have established a living trust.

Many, many people choose the first alternative, which is usually a choice by default. That is the one of doing nothing. This means that if you die without a will and without ever having an attorney make an analysis of your estate, then you have died *intestate*. This simply means you have died without a will or other testamentary documentation. If you die intestate, then your state of legal residence has a predetermined course of action to follow in distributing your estate. This system is known as *intestate succession*. It determines, according to the general feelings of society and the legislature of your state, the way in which your assets will be distributed (i.e., first to your spouse, then to your children, then to other relatives or descendants). When the person who dies is married, the process of intestate succession *does not avoid* probate at the death of the husband nor at the death of the wife, nor a double taxation on the assets which are taxed when the surviving spouse in turn dies, owning all the assets, and is taxed. At the end of this chapter you will find a facetious example of this alternative.

The second alternative estate plan is to draft a simple will. A simple will is one that merely states at the death of the maker of the will that she desires for all her assets be distributed outright to her beneficiaries (i.e., her husband, children, or charity). A simple will requires that a probate administration be incurred to determine if, in fact, this is the last will and testament of the decedent. Once the probate court has determined that this is the last will and testament, then it notifies creditors and carries out the intent of the decedent in regard to the transfer of her assets after all her debts have been paid according to the terms of her last will and testament. A last will and testament does not avoid probate at the death of the first member of the marriage, nor does it avoid probate at the death of the other. And it does not avoid the double taxation which will arise when the assets of the first spouse to die are included in the estate of the surviving spouse when he or she subsequently transfers the assets to the children.

The third alternative estate plan is to place all of your cash assets in what is known as a "Totten trust." A Totten trust is one where the decedent, during her lifetime, placed cash assets in her name with the words "in trust for" following her name. For instance, a typical Totten trust is where a mother takes $10,000 and places it into a savings and loan in the mother's name, Jane Doe, in trust for her son, Jimmy Doe. During the lifetime of the mother, she will pay all the income taxes on any interest or income earned. And she will have the right to revoke this manner of holding title so that she has complete flexibility in control of her assets. But when the mother passes away, then it can be shown and proven that the intent of the mother was that, upon her demise, this $10,0000 savings account be transferred to her son, Jimmy Doe. The advantage of a Totten trust is that the assets in the trust do not go through probate but are distributed outright to the beneficiary (her son, Jimmy Doe) without the necessity of a probate administration. However, because the mother retained all the ownership and control of that account during her lifetime, the entire amount of $10,000 is included in the mother's estate when she dies and is therefore taxed.

A fourth alternative estate plan is to hold title to the estate in *joint tenancy*. Joint tenancy is a means of taking title to property where the parties to the joint tenancy may contribute equally or unequally. The distinguishing characteristic of joint tenancy is that upon the death of the first joint tenant, any assets held in that joint tenancy arrangement are, by operation of law, distributed outright to the surviving joint tenant. This process is called *right of survivorship.* This arrangement is by statute in most states but does not replace the need for a will.

A typical example of a joint tenancy arrangement would be where a mother, Mary Doe, and a daughter, Sally, place $20,000 into a savings account which reads, "Mary Doe and Sally Doe as Joint Tenants." The consequences of owning any assets in joint tenancy are that upon the death of either Mary or Sally, title to the assets held in joint tenancy immediately vests in the surviving joint tenant upon the principle of right of survivorship. The advantage of holding an asset in joint tenancy is that in most states joint tenancy will avoid the necessity of probate administration on any assets that are held in that manner. But in a situation where a husband and wife hold assets in joint tenancy, there are limitations. If the husband and wife are fatally injured in a common disaster, technically they don't die simultaneously. Their assets will not got through probate at the death of the first spouse but they *will* go through a probate at the death of the surviving spouse whether that is moments or months later. Also, joint tenancy does not avoid the *double taxation* which we have been discussing which occurs when the assets of the first spouse to die are *added* and included to the assets of the estate of the surviving spouse. When the surviving spouse winds up owning a very large estate, the assets are taxed at a *higher* tax bracket.

The fifth means of establishing one's estate plan is through the use of a *testamentary trust.* In the trust, there are three entities, or people: a trustor, a trustee and a beneficiary. The trustor is the person who desires to create the trust. Until that trust is executed (when the trustor dies), the trustor has all legal and beneficial title to her assets. The trustor establishes a trust by engaging an attorney to draft the trust document.

Then she transfers her assets to the trustee. The trustee is the person who has legal title to the assets and is vested with the responsibility of managing, controlling, accounting for, protecting, and investing the assets of the trustor for the beneficiary or beneficiaries. The beneficiaries are the people who receive the benefits of the trust according to the intent and desires of the trustor.

A testamentary trust is a trust that you create to take effect at your death. You draft a will and in your will, you include your trust. Your will states that upon your death it is your intent that rather than distribute your assets outright at the conclusion of the probate administration, you intend that these assets be held in trust by a bank, title insurance, or trust company, or another individual or entity of your choice. You designate that the trustee will hold these assets, protect and invest them to the benefit of the people that you have wished to derive the benefits from your assets. One reason you might do this is that, for one reason or another, you feel your beneficiaries are not yet of sufficient age, maturity, and sophistication to handle your assets. Or you may feel that the individual or institutional trustee which you name in the trust is better suited to handle the investments for the benefit of a spouse or children than they may be themselves. As you probably noticed, we mentioned that the trust goes into effect at your death but that the assets are distributed upon the completion of probate. The testamentary trust, because it is included in a will, goes through probate. But, for the first time in any of our examples, we see that a testamentary trust has the advantage of avoiding the double tax which will occur at the death of the surviving spouse when he or she has had added to his or her assets all of the assets which he or she inherited from the spouse. So the testamentary trust may avoid double taxation but does not avoid probate.

Finally, we have the sixth and last method for estate planning. It is the one that we feel is the most effective. This is the *living trust*. The legal term for a living trust is "Inter Vivos," Latin words which mean "among the living." This is a trust which is established to take effect during your own lifetime.

A trust is created while you are alive and a trustee of your choice is named to handle the assets in your trust while you are alive. This gives you the opportunity to see how the trust works while you are still living. You can make certain that the trustee is, in fact, going to do a good job. And you can iron out any problems that may arise. Obviously, you can't iron out any problems when you are dead. For this reason, a testamentary trust is a gamble that the trustee you've named is, in fact, going to do a good job. The advantage of a living trust is that you may control the trust and get it operating while you are alive. And you are relatively assured that it will continue to operate efficiently after you have passed away.

The advantages of the living trust over a testamentary trust are that the living trust avoids all probate at the death of the first spouse and avoids all probate at the death of the other spouse. It also avoids the double taxation which we have talked about earlier. It is the only way we know of, short of dying without assets or leaving all assets to charity, that a-voids all probate at the death of each spouse and double taxa-tion. None of the other five methods does this.

Living trusts are not just advantageous to married couples. Some tax savings can be arranged for the heirs of single per-sons. Even in situations where there are no tax advantages, the avoidance of probate and all the inconvenience to the beneficiaries makes the living trust worthwhile.

Living trusts are flexible instruments which can and should be designed to meet the intentions of the person or the couple that established the trust. For this reason, it is difficult to de-scribe a typical trust but we will do our best. Let us say for the purposes of this example that you are Jane Doe and your husband is John Doe. An attorney has drafted a trust naming you both as co-trustees while you are alive. It is interesting to know that you do not have to choose somebody else as the trustee of your own trust. The Internal Revenue Service refers to the type of trust which you have established as a *Grantor Trust*. All the income which is earned by the combined assets of you and your husband during your lifetime will be taxed on your regular federal and state income tax returns just as if you have not established this trust. In setting up the trust, you took all the assets which you desired to include in the trust and transferred these assets so that the title now reads "Jane Doe and John Doe as co-trustees of the Doe family trust." During your lifetime this trust is revocable. You may revoke it at any time you desire. Upon the death of one of you, you may name a bank or other trustee to serve as the trustee of your trust. At this time, however, the trust must file IRS information tax returns. This means that for the first time, whoever is named as the trustee of your trust must now file a federal and state fiduciary tax return, but the trust does not pay any taxes. You merely report to the IRS that you have a trust and that the income is being reported on your personal tax returns if it is distributed to you outright. The advantage of the living trust, besides avoiding all probate and double taxation, is that if you and your husband die in a common disaster, a trust for the benefit of your children is immediately established.

Obviously, if you and your spouse were to die simultaneously, you would want to have made the best provisions possible for your children. Depending on the ages and circumstances of the children, you might wish that your estate be divided into equal trusts. On the other hand, if several of your children have reached majority, have completed their education, and are successfully established and financially secure, you may wish to give them a lesser amount than minor children who will still need substantial support to complete their education. It is possible for you to make very specific provisions in your trust. You may feel that even after your child has reached the age of eighteen you do not wish for that child to have the entire inheritance. You may stipulate that the child receive a portion of the inheritance at age twenty-five, another portion at age thirty, and the rest of the trust at age thirty-five. Many parents feel that it will take a substantial period of time before their children can competently and successfully handle their inheritance. Another form of flexibility which might be encompassed in your living trust would be provisions that the trustee pay for the educational and medical expenses of a child no matter what those expenses come to while in addition giving a certain percentage of the income from the trust over to the child on a regular basis. Another way to set up the trust might be to only have actual expenses subtracted from the trust so that whatever savings remain would continue to produce interest.

So, getting back to our example of Jane and John Doe, by virtue of the arrangements that you have made in establishing a living trust, you have accomplished several goals. If both of you should come to a sudden and untimely death, you have distributed things to your children not in a lump sum, which could be unprofessionally managed or squandered, but rather you have given them their estates in reasonable portions so that if they lose or misinvest one portion, hopefully they will have learned their lessons and will have several more portions distributed to them which they will properly manage and protect.

If you have thought about it, you will realize that all six of the previously mentioned methods of distributing your estate deal with the possibility that you are going to die. If you know for a fact that you are never going to die, you have nothing to worry about! There is, however, another way to avoid probate and death taxes. This would be to die with nothing in your name. If you are able to spend everything while you are alive and you have nothing left when you die, there's nothing left to be taxed. This is nice if you happen to know exactly when you are going to die and you have nobody you are particularly interested in having benefit from your estate.

A common way that many people attempt to do estate planning is to transfer their wealth to their beneficiaries while they are alive. We would like to point out a few things to people who attempt to do this. If you transfer things away and die within three years, the 1976 Tax Reform Act states that the value of those things transferred within three years of death shall definitely be brought back and included in your estate and fully taxed as though a transfer had never even been made. Another problem with this form of estate planning is that since you can't really be too sure when you will die, there is always the possibility that you will distribute your entire estate only to find yourself having to approach your children and friends and ask for some of it back to continue your own support. Transferring things away before death is not necessarily good if it renders the transferor insolvent or in such an insecure financial position that she becomes dependent upon her children for income just because she has transferred all of her wealth to the children.

If, after what we have said, you are still intent on giving away some gifts out of your estate prior to your death, let us propose the basic ways this should be done. If it is your intention to transfer assets away prior to death, then the proper way to do it is to take advantage of the tax exclusions which would result in transferring gifts away tax free. And, above all, remember to wait three years before dying after making that transfer! Our tax laws allow a transferor to transfer $3,000 per donee without having any tax consequences. Therefore, a mother and father combined could give $6,000 per year to their children and pay no federal gift or transfer taxes on that transfer. The 1976 Tax Reform Act has modified the tax consequences for one who wishes to give an amount larger than $3,000 per donee. After 1981 an individual may give $175,000 of assets to his beneficiaries tax free but at death the amount which he would own would be fully taxable in his estate without any exemptions or limitations.

We are sorry that in a book of this size we are unable to give more attention to the complex and very important issue of estate planning. We hope that from this chapter you have been able to look a little more analytically at some unpleasant subjects. Hopefully, this will be a case where you will discover that an ounce of prevention is worth a pound of cure. Remember, you can't take it with you and it sure would be nice if your heirs didn't think you did!

ESTATE PLANNING CONFIDENTIAL QUESTIONNAIRE

Personal and family Information

1. Client's Full Name: _____Birthdate:_____
2. Spouse's Full Name: _____Birthdate:_____
3. Address: _____Telephone:_____
4. Date of Marriage:_____Place of Marriage: _____
5. Children of Present Marriage:

   Full Name   *Birthdate*   *City & State*

   _____
   _____

6. Spouses of Children of Present Marriage:

   Name of Child   Name of Spouse:

   _____
   _____

7. Grandchildren of Present Marriage:

   Name of Child   *Name of Grandchild*

   _____
   _____

8. Client's Parents if Living:

   Mother:_____ Father: _____
9. Spouse's Parents if Living:

   Mother:_____ Father: _____
10. Occupation:

    Husband: _____ Wife:_____
11. Social Security Number: Husband _____Wife_____
12. Date of Present Will: _____Residence at execution: _____
13. Have you been married previously? Husband:___Wife:___

    (If yes, complete the information below)

    Husband

    Name of Previous Spouse: _____

    Date of Death or Divorce: _____

    Title Location and Case Number of the Probate

    or Divorce Court: _____

    Wife

    Name of Previous Spouse: _____

    Date of Death or Divorce: _____

    Title, Location and Case Number of the Probate

    or Divorce Court: _____

14. Children of Previous Marriage:
    Husband's Children
Full Name	*Birthdate*	*City & State*

    Wife's Children
Full Name	*Birthdate*	*City & State*

15. Spouses of Children of Previous Marriage:
Name of Child	*Name of Spouse*

16. Grandchildren of Previous Marriage:
Name	*Age*	*Parent's Name*

17. Location of Safe Deposit Box(es):
Bank	*Location*	*Who has access*

18. Banking Affiliation:
    Client: _____ Spouse: _____

19. Financial and Legal Advisors:
    Client
Accountant	*Attorney*	*Life Insurance*	*Stock Broker*	*Other*

    Spouse

Assets and Liabilities (Attach Schedule if you need more space)

1. Real Property:

Description	*Location*	*Date Acquired*	*How Title Held*	*Fair Market Value*

2. Stocks and Bonds, Certificates of Deposit:

Description	No. of Shares	Date Acquired	How Title Held	Fair Market Value

3. Life Insurance

Company	Policy Number	Face Amount	Owner	Beneficiary	Date Acquired

4. Liquid Funds—Cash, Savings & Checking Accounts:

Institution	Type of Account	How Title Held	Account No.

5. Business:
   Name of Sole Proprietorship
   Partnership or Corporation: _____
   Location: _____ Date Business Began: _____
   How Title Held: _____ Percent of Ownership: ___

6. Tangible Personal Property:

Description	Fair Market Value	How Title Held	Date Acquired

   Jewelry

   Household Furnishings & Clothing

   Automobiles, Boats, Motor Homes

7. Trusts:
   Trustor:_____ Trustee:_____
   Beneficiary: _____ Date of Instrument:_____
   Amount of Income:_____ Amount of Corpus: _____

8. Anticipated Inheritances:

	From Whom	Amount	When Expected
Client:			
Spouse:			

9. Other Assets (Attach Schedule)
10. Liabilities: (Notes, Mortgages, Judgments)

	Liability	Amount	Institution Received
Client:			
Spouse:			

11. Gifts:

	Donee	Description	Amount
Client:			
Spouse:			

Alone

If you think dying without a will is fine, since there are already laws on the books looking out for you, carefully consider one writer's facetious will, as interpreted from the California State Statutes.

MY LAST WILL
DRAWN BY THE STATE OF CALIFORNIA

Being of sound mind and memory, I declare this to be my last Will.

FIRST: I give to my children two-thirds (⅔) of all my non-community property, and to my wife, what is left. It is her duty to support my children out of her share.

SECOND: I appoint my wife as guardian of my children. But as a safeguard, she shall report to the Probate Court each year and give an accounting of how, why, and where she spent my children's money. As a further safeguard, my wife must purchase a Performance Bond to guarantee that she uses proper judgment in handling investing, and spending my children's money.

THIRD: If my wife dies before me, and any of my children are minors, I do not wish to name a guardian to care for my minor children; rather I hope my relatives and friends will get together and select that guardian by mutual agreement. If they do not agree on a guardian, I direct the Probate Court to make the choice. If the Court wishes, it may appoint a stranger.

FOURTH: Under existing tax laws, there are certain legal ways to lower death taxes. Since I prefer to have my money used for governmental purposes rather than for the benefit of my wife and children, I direct that no effort be made to lower taxes.

IN WITNESS THEREOF, I have set my hand to this, my Last Will, this date now uncertain.

_____
TESTATOR

RESOURCES

Books About Divorce

Baskin, Henry and Kiel-Friedman, Sonya, *I've Had It, You've Had It (Advice on Divorce from a Lawyer and a Psychologist)* Los Angeles: Nash Publishing, 1974, 135 pp.
> A sort of advice column style book with representative individual quotes followed by a commentary from each author. Makes you realize you're not alone.

Berson, Barbara and Bova, Ben, *Survival Guide for the Suddenly Single.* New York: St. Martin's Press, 1974, 213 pp.
> A lighthearted optimistic look at the practicalities following separation and divorce. How to handle sex, children, money, friends, relatives, jobs, lawyers and setting new goals. Each of the authors was married for over fifteen years.

Bradley, Buff; Berman, Jan; Suid, Murray; and Suid, Roberta, *Single: Living Your Own Way.* Reading, Mass. Addison-Wesley Publishing Company, 1977, 184 pp.
> A really great resource book, full of candor, humor and insight. In Part I eleven single people tell their own stories about living alone. Part II focuses on the everyday problems and concerns of the single life. Eating alone, traveling, loneliness, sex, money, work and recreation are talked about by people who have learned how to cope. You'll enjoy this book tremendously. It will give you some courage and perspective to turn a "dismal alternative" into a vibrant possibility for growth and fulfillment.

Braudy, Susan, *Between Marriage and Divorce: A Woman's Diary.* New York: William Morrow and Company, Inc., 1975, 252 pp.
> A two-year diary by a New York Ms: editor and writer in her late twenties following her divorce after six years of marriage.

Cuse, Arthur, *Financial Guideline: Divorce.* Los Angeles: Guideline Publishing Co., 1971, 152 pp.
> Written by an independent financial consultant, this book deals with the financial aspects of divorce: how to determine the costs, how to prepare, and how to save your assets. Contains excellent

factual information and advice on dealing with attorneys, accountants, alimony, child support, property settlement, bank accounts, credit and charge cards, community and separate property. Highly recommended if any substantial property is involved, this is the best book of its kind we have found.

Edwards, Marie and Hoover, Eleanor, *The Challenge of Being Single (For Divorced, Widowed, Separated and Never-Married Men and Women)*. Los Angeles: J. P. Tarcher, Inc., 1974, 235 pp.
An outgrowth of Marie Edwards' work as a psychologist with singles and marrieds in personal growth and encounter groups, this book looks constructively at the advantages and disadvantages of living alone in a society that values "pairing." You will get some interesting insights from shared experiences.

Epstein, Joseph, *Divorced in America—Marriage in an Age of Possibility*. New York: E. P. Dutton &Co., 1974, 318 pp.
For the mature, intelligent and sensitive, this book is an oasis. The author, divorced after ten years of marriage and awarded custody of his two sons, gives full recognition to the knowledge that divorce after a lengthy marriage, when children are involved, is an incredibly complex process, legally, psychologically and socially. You will not find any easy answers, because there are none. You will find eloquence, wisdom, understanding and, perhaps, solace. The book may not appeal to all in its conservative, somewhat chauvinistic approach, but, all in all, it's the best available.

Fisher, Esther Oshiver, *Divorce: The New Freedom. A Guide to Divorcing and Divorce Counseling*. New York: Harper & Row, 1974, 196 pp.
Divorce counseling is discussed and illustrated with case histories. Dr. Fisher separates the divorce process into three separate and distinct phases: predivorce, the divorce itself, and postdivorce (the most difficult). Practical help is given through each phase.

Fuller, Jan, *Space (The Scrapbook of My Divorce)*. New York: Arthur Fields Books, Inc., 1973.
Excerpts from the personal diary of Jan Fuller (a pseudonym) written during the three month period following her final divorce decree. Not all marriages were like Jan's (seven years

and two sons) but you will identify with the ambivalence of her emotions. She expresses them beautifully.

Gardner, Richard A., M.D., *The Boys and Girls Book about Divorce*. New York: Science House, Inc., 1970, 158 pp.
This book is geared toward middle grade school to junior high school age kids and directed to the child whose mother has custody. No-nonsense talk with chapters about divorce, blaming one parent or another (or yourself), the love of a parent for a child, anger and its uses, fear of being left alone, how to get along better with your divorced mother/father/parents living apart/stepparent, and other problems.

Gardner, Richard A., M.D., *The Parents Book about Divorce*. Garden City: Doubleday & Company, Inc., 1977, 357 pp.
An up-to-date and indispensable guide for mothers who want to make their children's emotional transition during divorce as easy as possible. The book discusses problems with children such as denial of the divorce, fear of abandonment, reconciliation preoccupations, sexual and identification problems, visitation and custody.

Grollman, Earl A. (editor), *Explaining Divorce to Children*. Boston: Beacon Press, 1969, 245 pp.
This book may not be very reassuring but it is a real eye-opener. It is the serious and compassionate attempt of nine experts on divorce from the fields of sociology, psychiatry, psychology, law, child study and the three major religions to deal with the child's fears, reactions and undermined sense of security resulting from divorce. It consistently and wholeheartedly considers the child's viewpoint and best interest.

Hunt, Morton and Hunt, Bernice, *The Divorce Experience*. New York: McGraw-Hill Book Company, 1977, 269 pp.
A brand new look at the way "formerly marrieds" are living today: how they work out their problems, how they interact and support one another, how and why they remarry. If you'd like some perspective and reassurance before stepping out in your new social role, be sure and give this book a glance. It can save you some awkward and worrisome moments.

Alone

Krantzler, Mel, *Creative Divorce. A New Opportunity for Personal Growth.* New York: M. Evans and Company, Inc., 1973, 268 pp.
One of the first to take a positive approach to the subject, this book outlines the divorce process from the death of a relationship, through grieving, to the rebirth of the individual.

Krantzler, Mel, *Learning to Love Again.* New York: Thomas Y. Crowell Company, 1977, 243 pp.
Written seven years after his own divorce, the author, a counselor in human relations, draws on his own personal and professional experience in discussing the four stages of learning to love again: (1) The Remembered-Pain Stage, (2) The Questing-Experimental Stage, (3) The Selective-Distancing Stage, and (4) The Creative-Commitment Stage. What promised to be an encouraging "sequel" is unbearably pompous and chauvinistic.

Moffett, Robert K. and Scherer, Jack F., L.L.B., L.L.M., *Dealing with Divorce.* Boston: Little, Brown and Company, 1976.
Written by attorneys, this book may be heavier reading than you feel like but it is well worth the trouble. It gives you sound, realistic advice on what you can expect during a divorce proceeding and how important it is to organize your thinking at a time when it may be extremely difficult to do so. Lots of information on grounds, alimony, child support and child custody.

Salk, Dr. Lee, *What Every Child Would Like Parents to Know about Divorce.* New York: Harper & Row, 1978, 149 pp.
A quick, plain-talk book written by the noted child psychologist and television personality, Dr. Lee Salk, who is himself a recently divorced parent with custody of his two children. The book draws from Salk's personal experience and has examples from his practice as a therapist.

Singleton, Mary Ann, *Life After Marriage. Divorce as a New Beginning.* New York: Stein and Day, 1974, 204 pp.
The author, married at twenty-two, divorced with two children after nine years of marriage, explains, ". . . I would not know that fearful woman I once was, hungering after security. . . I wanted to say to other women: *so can you,* and that is why I

wrote this book." A book full of zest, perseverance, low-key inspiration and lots of good practical advice, particularly if you have kids!

Books About Widowhood

Agee, James, *A Death In the Family*. Bantam Books (edition), 1969, 318 pages.
This is a novel, It is well-written and gets the reader in touch with the family dynamics surrounding the sudden accidental death of a young husband and father of two children.

Caine, Lynn, *Widow*. Bantam Book (edition), 1975, 183 pages.
This has been the most popular and controversial book on widowhood that has come out in years. Lynn Caine lost her husband to cancer. She explores her own emotional trauma which followed with rare candor. One of her best suggestions is a day of contingency for married couples to sit down once a year and honestly communicate legal and financial expectations "should anything happen to me."

Colgrove, Melba, Ph.D., Bloomfield, Harold H., M.D. and McWilliams, Peter. *How To Survive the Loss of a Love*, Leo Press, dist. by Simon & Schuster, 1976, 131 pages.
This is a very popular and sound primer to help people suffering any loss. Interspersed among the sound, well-written advice on handling one's grief, are beautiful poems. This small book makes a great gift for someone going through divorce or widowhood.

Decker, Beatrice, as told to Gladys Kooiman, *After the Flowers Have Gone*, Zondervan, 1973, 184 pages.
This book was written by a widow who organized a national organization called T.H.E.O.S. which stands for They Help Each Other Spiritually. She shares her own widowhood experience as well as what she has learned through the participation in her program.

Kreis, Bernadine and Pattie, Alice, *Up From Grief*, The Seabury Press, 1969, 146 pages.
This has been a classic primer on grief for the lay person for over

a decade. It is simple, well-written and helps a person suffering through grief by making the psychological process so understandable.

LeShan, Eda, *Learning to Say Goodbye*, When a Parent Dies, MacMillan Publishing Co., Inc., 1976, 85 pages.
The introduction to this book states "... a child can live through anything, so long as he or she is told the truth and is allowed to share with loved ones the natural feelings that people have when they are suffering." The book is geared to children but is valuable to adults. It could be a valuable tool for a whole family to share when working through a grief.

Marshall, Catherine, *To Live Again*, Spire Books, 1972, 336 pages.
This very popular old book was written by the widow of Peter Marshall, chaplain to the United States Senate. Widows of religious bent often go on to read all her other books after they have sampled her marvelous warmth and understanding from this episode of loss.

Pike, Diane Kennedy, *Life is Victorious*, Simon and Schuster, 1976, 209 pages.
This book is written by the widow of Bishop James Pike. Her candor is almost embarrassing and her philosophy of growth through grief truly encouraging. Because of her own experience and growth, she has organized an international program called The Love Project. After reading this book, you may subscribe to the tenets that she explains and wish to beome involved.

Start, Clarissa, *On Becoming a Widow*, Family Library, 1973, 124 pages.
In this book, Clarissa Start gently shares her own experience and the insight she gained from it. The book is short and sweet and well-liked by those who read it.

Tanner, Ira J., *The Gift of Grief*, Hawthorn Books, Inc., 1976, 167 pages.
The cover on this book, appropriately enough, is a bright rainbow. The author, a marriage and family and child counselor, candidly counsels the reader about the many griefs we all en-

counter and how to handle grief. The best thing about this book is the recognition of so many other grief-causing events besides death.

Creative Widowhood Adjustment Cassettes
Creative Divorce Adjustment Cassettes
Specially recorded messages for stress reduction and adjustment. Contact:
Ann Sturgis, Ph.D.
Stress Management Training Institute .
2240 Caminito Preciosa Sur
La Jolla, California, 92037

Publications About Money Management

Black, Joan, *The Modern Woman's Key to Financial Security* California: Major, 1975.
A good basic book written especially for a woman planning her financial future.

Barron's Weekly. Available by subscription, Newstands or write Dow Jones & Co. 22 Cortland St., New York 10007.
The best weekly newspaper written for the financial community.

Engle, Louis, *How to Buy Stocks* 5th edition revised, Boston Little & Brown, 1971.
A down to earth guide on understanding the stock and bond markets.

Fisher, Philip A., *Conservative Investors Sleep Well* New York Harper & Row, 1975.
A sophisticated guide for the investor who wants to accumulate a carefully balanced portfolio.

Hardy, Colburn C., *Dun & Bradstreet's Guide to Your Investments* Thomas Crowell Co. New York, 1978.
A yearly paperback publication containing all the current statistics and information on the world of investments.

Homer, Sidney, *Bond Buyer's Primer* Salomon Bros. & Hutzler, 1968.
   This book is a must for anyone who owns or is considering buying corporate or municipal bonds.

Moody's, A financial newspaper. Write to Moody's Investors Service, 99 Church Street New York, N.Y.
   This is a highly specialized financial newspaper.

Nelson, Paula, *The Joy of Money*, Stein and Day, 1975, 227 pages.
   This book will guide one swiftly and easily into the idea that financial freedom can be a real possibility and joy to women.

Porter, Sylvia, *Money Book* New York Doubleday & Company, Inc. 1975.
   A must for everyone's library. A dictionary of financial terms.

Rodda, W. H., *The Question and Answer Insurance Deskbook* Prentice Hall, 1975.
   A good resource book on the various types of insurance.

Rukeyser, M. S. *Common Sense of Money and Investments* New York Doubleday & Co., Inc., 1975.
   An excellent general book that discusses good hedges against inflation.

Standard & Poor's Stock Guide, published monthly.
   Rates some 5000 companies. Also offers statistics about these companies. Write to Standard and Poor's Corp., 345 Hudson Street, New York, 10014.

The Wall Street Journal, the best all around financial daily newspaper.
   It can be purchased at newsstands or for a suscription write: Dow Jones and Co., Inc. 22 Courtland St., New York 10007.

Weisenberger Financial Services Investment Companies. Issued annually.
   Write to 5 Hanover Square, New York. This book is the best resource book for information on mutual funds.

INDEX

Accountant
    attorney as, 17
    for valuation of property, 36
Address of Widowed Persons
    Service, 81
Administrator and admin-
    istratrix. *See* Executors and ad-
    ministrators
Advice, sources of, 10, 11
Age and credit rating, 160
Agency bonds, 140, 141
Agriculture, investments in, 136
Ahern, D., 147
Alimony. *See* Support of spouse
Amnesia and grief, 54
Amortization of debt, 92
Annuities, 175
    estate tax on, 74
Apartments, investing in,
    119–121
Appraisers, 36
Art, valuation of, 36
Assets and liabilities
    attorneys requiring, 29
    division of, 34–37
    and net worth, 88–95
    for probate, 69, 70
Attorneys
    choice of, 13–24
    depositions by, 36
    documents required by, 30
    fees, *see* Attorney's fees
    information for, 29
    and probate, 57, 58
    and real estate investments, 123
Attorney's fees, 19, 20
    changing attorneys, statement
        on, 23
    in estate administration, 79, 80
Automobiles
    Blue Book value of, 90

expenses, 96
insurance for, 170, 171

Bank accounts
    automatic savings plans, 105
    estate administration inventory
        of, 60
    flexibility of, 136–138
Bar Association and disputes with
    attorney, 23
Beneficial property, 74
Best interests of the child in cus-
    tody cases, 46
Bitterness
    and divorce, 5
    and trials, 38
Blue Book value of automobile, 90
Bodily injury liability insurance,
    170
Bonds
    securities, *see* Securities
    surety bonds for executors,
        66–68
Brokers
    and advice, 123
    insurance, 176, 177
    stockbrokers, 146, 147
Budgets, 98–107
Burial ceremony, 52–54
Businesses, valuation of, 36

Capital gains taxes, 115, 128, 129
Careers, goals of, 28
Cash
    budgeting of, 101
    and net worth, 89
Catastrophic expectations, 85
CPA, attorney as, 17
Certified public accountant, at-
    torney as, 17
Changes after separation, 7, 8

Alone

Changing attorneys, 22, 23
Checking accounts. *See* Bank accounts
Child support, 34, 43–45
  and credit, 162
  temporary support, 95
Children
  custody, *see* Custody of children
  and estate tax, 75
  grief of, 11, 12
  medical insurance for, 173
  and pressures, 26
  and simultaneous death, 189
  support, *see* Child support
Claims adjusters, 177, 178
Claims against estate. *See* Creditors' claims
Clergy and grief, 9
College education and child support, 44
Collision insurance, 170
Commingling property, 35
Common stock, 142, 143
Communication with attorney, 21
Community property and co-signing credit accounts, 161
  and credit, 159–161
  disputes over, 94, 95
  estate administration inventory of, 60
  and estate tax, 73
  identification of, 34–36
Complaint for divorce, filing of, 32, 33
Comprehensive insurance, 170
Condominiums, 117–119
  insurance for, 171
Confidants. *See* Friends
Contempt and child support, 44, 45
Contested divorces and attorney's fees, 20

Contingent fee contracts with attorneys, 20
Convertible bonds, 144
Convertible preferred stock, 143
Cooperative apartments, 117–119
Co-signing credit accounts, 160, 161
Cost of living and support, 44
Counsel. *See* Attorneys
Counselors
  attorney as, 17, 18
  for grief, 9
  investments, 145–148
  referrals, 9, 10
Court appearance for divorce, 40, 41
Courtesy titles and credit, 159
Courtroom experience of attorney, 16, 17
Credit, 155–165
  agencies to contact, 165
  and co-signing, 160, 161
  debts on, 92, 155–165
  poor risks, 157, 158
  refusal of, 165
Credit rating, 156
  and age, 160
Credit reporting, 163, 164
Credit unions, accounts in, 138
Creditors' claims
  and estate administration, 64
  and probate, 68, 69
Crying, 2
  and men, 3
Custody of children, 45–47
  fees of attorney in, 20
  punishment, tool for, 5
  temporary orders for, 34

Death certificates, 53
  estate administration inventory including, 60

206